BERIO

Oxford Studies of Composers (20)

BERIO

DAVID OSMOND-SMITH

Oxford   New York

OXFORD UNIVERSITY PRESS

1991

Oxford University Press, Walton Street, Oxford OX2 6DP

Oxford New York Toronto
Delhi Bombay Calcutta Madras Karachi
Petaling Jaya Singapore Hong Kong Tokyo
Nairobi Dar es Salaam Cape Town
Melbourne Auckland
and associated companies in
Berlin Ibadan

Oxford is a trade mark of Oxford University Press

Published in the United States
by Oxford University Press, New York

British Library Cataloguing in Publication Data
Osmond-Smith, David
Berio.—(Oxford studies of composers).
1. Italian symphonies. Berio, Luciano, 1925–
I. Title II. Series
784.184092
ISBN 0–19–315478–1
ISBN 0–19–315455–2 (pbk.)

Library of Congress Cataloging in Publication Data
Osmond-Smith, David.
— (Oxford studies of composers; 24)
Includes bibliographical references and index.
1. Berio, Luciano, 1925– ·—Criticism and interpretation.
I. Title. II. Series.
ML410.B4968O55 1990
780'.92—dc20
[B] 90–7368
ISBN 0–19–315478–1
ISBN 0–19–315455–2 (pbk.)

Set by Hope Services (Abingdon) Ltd
Printed in Great Britain by
Biddles Ltd, Guildford and King's Lynn

PREFACE

This book is indebted to many people. Firstly to Luciano Berio himself, who has been generous with time and information, and suggested a number of valuable emendations. Then to the late Cathy Berberian, whose recollections helped to shape Chapter V; to Nicola Bernardini of Tempo Reale in Florence, without whose advice the technical portions of Chapter VI would have lacked clarity; to Robin Anderson and Kim Summershield of Universal Edition's London office, and to Silvio Cerutti of Suvini Zerboni for unstinting support, and the loan of many scores.

The Bibliography is a selective one, and includes only those items that are particularly germane to the text of the book. If the Work List represents an advance upon previous attempts, this is due in substantial measure to the scholarship of Marsha Berman, who generously shared the fruits of her own research even though this has yet to appear in print. But I must also warmly thank Elisabeth Knessl of Universal Edition, Vienna, Rossana Dalmonte, Roberto Leydi, Ward Swingle, Walter Trampler, and Willem Vos for their help in elucidating points of detail.

D.O.-S.

Brighton, 1989

CONTENTS

LIST OF MUSIC EXAMPLES

Grateful thanks are due to the following publishers for permission to reproduce music examples:

Edizioni Suvini Zerboni, Milan: Examples I.2, I.3, II.2, II.3, II.4, III.1, III.2, and III.3.

Universal Edition: III.4, III.6, III.7, III.8, IV.1, IV.3, IV.4, IV.5, IV.6, V.1, VI.1, VI.2, and VII.5.

I
MUSICAL APPRENTICESHIP

Only once in the course of a long career was Luciano Berio visited by doubts about his musical vocation. Born and raised by the sea, at the age of eleven he decided that his future lay in working on it, as captain of his own boat. That odyssey was not to be realized, but another took its place: one equally accomodating of unquenchable curiosity and a taste for wide horizons. Even now Berio will echo the aspirations of his adolescence, and describe his music as a voyage that has taken in many ports of call. Perhaps that metaphor places in its just perspective one of the more singular aspects of his work. His appetite for drawing creative consequences from a wide range of disciplines has been formidable —phonetics, structural anthropology, and more consistently ethnomusicology, electro-acoustic research, and the experimental traditions of literature and theatre have all at one point or another suggested new directions in his work. Undoubtedly such excursions as these have caught the imagination of a wide range of listeners (though they also reduced one respected critic, Fedele D'Amico, to the sweeping, but much-repeated expedient of describing Berio as an 'omnivore'). But they would hardly have sustained lasting attention were they not interacting with a musical language of singular vitality and directness.

For all its rich surface detail, Berio's music tends to root itself in processes that are relatively simple, and can thus offer access to the newcomer without starving the experienced listener of fresh discoveries. The student of his scores will soon discover that even this diversity of surface detail is often achieved by such long-established cornerstones of musical craftsmanship as the transformation of pre-established materials, or the permutation of limited resources. Berio's music owes much of its impact to this ability to engage the interest of all sorts and conditions of musician. This study therefore aims to pursue Berio on what Calvino described for him as 'the sea of music',[1] and to treat the various ports of call, so tempting to commentators, as adjuncts to the long sea voyage.

There is considerable continuity in the development of Berio's musical concerns. (He once remarked that 'like a good Ligurian, I never throw anything away'.) So that although this study does not attempt a detailed biography, an understanding of his early development sets many later features of his music into perspective. The Berio family had been active as professional musicians around the towns of the Ligurian coastline for a number of years.[2] Berio's somewhat formidable grandfather, Adolfo (1847–1942), had pursued a long career as organist and composer in Oneglia, a small town near Imperia. His music responded to the immediate needs of his environment: masses and dance-music. It is perhaps not without significance that Berio, when discussing his family, shows a greater sympathy for this absolutely practical relationship with the surrounding world than he does with the more ambitious aspirations of his father, Ernesto (1883–1966).[3] Ernesto Berio had studied at the Milan Conservatorio, as his son was to do after him, and he had also taken composition lessons from Pizzetti. When he returned to Oneglia, it was to pursue a wide and rather engaging range of activities: he presided at the piano in the local cinema, played in dance-bands, and organized regular chamber music evenings at home, as well as attending to his duties as a church organist. But at the same time he was writing music that plainly aspired to a wider and a more sophisticated audience than Oneglia could provide: polished settings for voice and piano, and a symphonic poem dedicated, much to his son's embarassment, to the 'heir of Augustus', Mussolini.

As might be expected in such an environment, Berio's musical education was early and thorough. His grandfather taught him the rudiments, and his father then took over, supervising his work in harmony and counterpoint, and his study of the piano. By the time he was eight or nine, Berio was sufficiently proficient to join in his father's chamber music evenings. His first attempt at composition came a few years later when, prompted by Romain Rolland's *roman fleuve* about an imaginary composer, *Jean-Christophe*, he tried his own hand at a *Pastorale* for piano (1937). But this was just one aspect of an all-round musical education: to this day, Berio retains a compelling sense of the links that bind together all aspects of musical activity, and views with scepticism those who choose to define themselves as 'composer', rather than as 'musician'.

Berio's particular concern for composition was brought into

sharper focus by the aftermath of an incident that took place in 1944. At that point in the war, Mussolini's Republic of Salò still held control of Liguria, and the 19-year-old Berio was called up to join the army being conscripted under its aegis. He complied with extreme reluctance: by now he viewed his father's naïve enthusiasm for Mussolini with vigorous distaste, and was tempted to follow friends who had joined the partisans, and had gone into hiding in the mountains. But aware of the consequences that this might have for his parents he temporized, and reported to the army at San Remo. The situation was chaotic: on his first day, without any previous instruction, he was given a loaded gun. As he was trying to understand how it worked, it blew up, severely injuring his right hand. After three gruelling months in a military hospital that no longer had medicines to treat his septic wounds, he faked a discharge and fled first to Milan, and then to Como to join the partisans.

But by now the war was coming to an end, so that in the autumn of 1945 Berio was able to enrol at the Milan Conservatorio. The Conservatorio ran a ten-year course, but his sound musical upbringing enabled him to take the fourth-year exam immediately, and join the fifth year.[4] His main instrument was to be the piano (with clarinet as second instrument), but it soon became plain that his hand injury was going to prevent a career as a keyboard player. So his six years as a student increasingly focused upon consolidating his technique as a composer. Up to his twentieth year he had completed only a handful of compositions, and had done so in an environment where any lively sense of recent musical history was lacking. Mussolini's regime was by no means as draconian in its suppression of radical and experimental traditions as was Nazi Germany's, but, for all that, musical life outside one or two cultural centres remained largely hostile to them. The adolescent Berio had been able to take his explorations of the chamber repertoire as far as Brahms and Dvořák during his father's musical evenings, and of opera as far as Puccini through radio broadcasts. But it was only now in post-war Milan that he was suddenly able to explore the music of his own century. His first encounter was with Milhaud's *La Mort d'un Tyran*, performed in Milan in October 1945, only a few months after Mussolini's body had been put on public display. (He was not to forget this work's combination of speaking chorus and percussion when he came to write *Passaggio*.) Then came Bartók's *Sonata for Two Pianos and*

3

Percussion, Stravinsky, and Hindemith. In 1946 he heard the first Milanese performance of Schoenberg's *Pierrot Lunaire*. At the time the experience left him baffled, but within a few years he was beginning to explore the scores of Schoenberg, Berg, and Webern with increasing interest.

But such explorations went hand in glove with a rigorous consolidation of technique. His father had given him a good working knowledge of harmony: this he now sought to complement by following the counterpoint course taught by Giulio Cesare Paribeni. This was hardly a popular choice. Often Berio and Paribeni were alone in class. But for Berio the experience was crucial: when discussing his own thoughts on musical pedagogy forty years later, he still gave pride of place to counterpoint.[5] Not that he was to prove a contrapuntist in the traditional sense. But counterpoint accustoms the listening musician to that exploratory and inventive mode of perception to which the mind resorts when dealing with several processes at once: a domain that Berio has explored insistently. And because it stretches one's sense of musical line, a counterpoint class is no mean preparation for the great arches of melody that run through Berio's later work.

Alongside his technical exercises for Paribeni, Berio began to produce a more steady flow of compositions. A *Petite Suite* for piano of 1947, which was to be Berio's first work to be performed in public (and has since been published by Universal Edition alongside works by Adolfo and Ernesto Berio), shows him discovering and assimilating a whole range of enthusiasms: Ravel, Prokofiev, and the neoclassical lingua franca of an older generation of Italian composers. Responding to these moments of fascination by active imitation—a process that he describes as 'exorcism'—was to provide the impetus for Berio's rapid development during his mid-twenties.

From Paribeni's counterpoint class Berio proceeded, in 1948, to Giorgio Ghedini's composition class, and thus came face to face with one of the major influences in his early career. Ghedini had come to the Milan Conservatorio in 1941, and during the next few years, when he was in his early fifties, had begun to write the works which established his permanent reputation. It was his generation that had been the first fully to appreciate the richness to the Italian baroque tradition, and during the 1930s his compositional style had shifted towards a neo-baroque idiom that made intelligent use of Stravinsky's example without thereby

4

losing its individuality. By common consent, that individuality rested largely upon Ghedini's handling of instrumental timbre and texture: the clear, cold, somewhat withdrawn sound-world that he created was almost without parallel in Italian music of the time.

Berio was to prove a rapid and eager student of Ghedini's skill in instrumentation, for by so doing he was filling one of the major gaps in his childhood education. The Italian provinces had never shown any great enthusiasm for the orchestral traditions of northern Europe, and the privations of the war years were such that Berio had only heard his first live orchestral concert at the age of 15. Now he advanced by leaps and bounds. The *Concertino* for clarinet (his own second instrument), concertante violin, celesta, harp, and strings of 1949 was his first work to achieve public performance apart from some piano pieces and a song. It already showed an assured grasp of idiomatic instrumental writing within a broadly neoclassical idiom, and reflected something of Berio's new-found fascination with the music of Stravinsky—an influence acknowledged quite openly in a *Magnificat* for two sopranos, chorus, two pianos, wind, and percussion that he wrote in the same year. Although this particular 'exorcism' was short-lived, hardly lasting beyond 1949, it left a permanent legacy of admiration for Stravinsky's musical craftsmanship.

Another permanent, but more tangible influence entered Berio's life at this time. Like many of his fellow music students, Berio earned his keep by accompanying and répétiteur work. At home in Oneglia he had been surrounded by singing, since his father gave frequent lessons. Now, at the Conservatorio, he accompanied singing classes, and having attended Giulini's conducting classes, began to take on conducting engagements in provincial opera houses. This long-standing immersion in the human voice, which was to bear such remarkable fruit a decade later, took on a more personal inflection in 1950. One of many jobs that he undertook that year was to accompany a young American-Armenian singer, Cathy Berberian, who was making a tape to support her application for a Fulbright Scholarship, so that she might continue her studies in Milan with Giorgina del Vigo. She won the scholarship, and within a few months she and Berio were married.

Although Ghedini in this, his most experimental period, made only occasional and tentative use of serial elements, he did not stand in the way of those more adventurous students who wished to come to grips with the legacy of the Second Viennese School. For Berio, as for several other young Italians of his generation, the most congenial route of access was through the music of Luigi Dallapiccola. The discipline and focus that Dallapiccola brought to the Italian lyrical tradition through serial techniques was a salutary corrective to the vagaries of neoclassical melody. Furthermore, his international stature had been reaffirmed by the first performances in 1949 (concert version) and 1950 (staged) of his one-act opera *Il prigioniero*, an event which even at the time was seen as marking a crucial step forward for Italian music after the war years. Berio had already immersed himself in a study of Dallapiccola's scores before he won a Koussevitzky Foundation bursary to study with the composer himself at the 1952 Berkshire Music Festival in Tanglewood, Massachusetts. Personal contact between them was cordial, but Berio learnt a good deal more of his compositional craft from the scores than from the man.

In those scores, Berio found a striking demonstration of the generative impetus that serial matrices can give to melodic invention. But he was never greatly enthralled by the impeccable musical geometries of the Webernian tradition, important though these were increasingly becoming to Dallapiccola himself. Indeed, Dallapiccola's pervasive use of canon was a feature that Berio found positively alienating. Therefore in those works produced between 1951 and 1954 in which Dallapiccola's melodic influence was most strongly felt, Berio took on board the exigencies of serial orthodoxy only in as much as they suited his creative needs. A typical case in point is *Chamber Music*, a setting of three early poems by James Joyce that he wrote for Cathy Berberian in 1953. At first glance it is clear that the series used for this work, set out in Ex. I.1, is designed to furnish lyrical opportunities rather than to expunge tonal and triadic echoes. Indeed, its inverted form

Ex. I.1 Pitch series for *Chamber Music*

retrogrades a series of groupings within the prime form (bracketed in Ex. I.1) so that melodic lines derived from it will sound as permutational variants of each other.

It is worth taking a closer look at how Berio put this series to use in the first setting, 'Strings in the Earth and Air', for the fluid approach to 'pre-compositional' systems in evidence here was to stay with him long beyond his involvement with serialism. The first few bars for voice and harp do not state the series as such, but instead employ the first five notes of the series (with pitches one and two switched) to create an autonomous structure whose retrogrades anticipate the final section of the song. But when clarinet and cello join them in bar 5 a clear serial counterpoint is established.

Ex. I.2 shows bars 5–7. If the voice's first entry is taken as P_0, as in Ex. I.1, then the harp accompanies with P_1, linked by its final note to P_2, the clarinet slowly plays P_4, and the cello R_0. But the voice does not sing all of P_0. Focusing upon the C$\sharp$, it misses out the subsequent B$\flat$, because the clarinet is sounding it, permutates the G and the F, and postpones the final C because, at 'the willows meet', it launches into P_4, whose second note is indeed C. Similarly, within the cello's statement of R_0 the B$\flat$ is again omitted, since that note is accounted for in the harp part. In other words, Berio is seeking out opportunities for melodic variation by organizing a serial polyphony that converges upon common pitches. For the rest of the first two verses, the mezzo-soprano's melody is built from fragments of the series, some continued by the instruments, some not, until the final line, 'Pale flowers . . .', where she sings a complete version of R_4, linked by its final note to R_1, hummed. Up to this point, the instruments have sustained a relatively complete serial polyphony, but now they too begin to build their textures, and even individual chords from fragments of the series. And it is thus that the last verse continues: a mosaic of serial fragments stuctured around the large-scale retrograde in the voice part that pivots upon the climactic *pp* at 'bent'.

The large-scale symmetries in evidence here (retrograde of serial fragments: $P_0 + P_4$: central serial fragments: $R_4 + R_1$: retrograde of serial fragments) owe much to the example of Dallapiccola, and are quite at odds with Berio's later sense of how time passes. But the detail is typical, in that when Berio establishes a reservoir of pre-compositional resources, he aims not at a self-denying ordinance, but a stimulus to the imagination that may

Ex. I.2 *Chamber Music I*, bars 5–7

well function as much by transgression as by observance. One consequence of this is that the analyst will often find in Berio's scores only hints or remnants of a 'system' which has in effect been consumed in the process of composition.

Of the pieces written under Dallapiccola's stylistic influence, the most explicit *hommage* is the *Cinque Variazioni* for piano of 1952–3. No theme is stated at the start of these variations, but during them the 'fratello' motif from Dallapiccola's *Il prigioniero* gradually moves to the foreground, until it dominates the coda— a telling reversal of the usual trajectory of a variation set. Although much of the material is free from specific serial ordering, it constantly reflects the lessons of the serial experience. For instance, Berio is alert to ways of using up the chromatic gamut. Ex. I.3 shows an extract from the first variation, followed by a transcription to a single octave.

Ex. I.3 *Cinque Variazioni*, p. 2, system 2

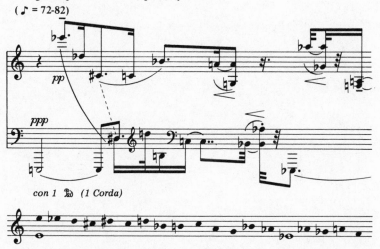

Such meandering chromatic ascents or descents are often used by Berio as a basis for melodic elaboration: examples occur through to the sixties, and there are many other instances in this work alone. (Indeed, when Berio temporarily establishes a conventional series in the *piu mosso* section of the second variation, this too follows an analogous shape.) They confirm a tendency to focus the listener's ear by working only with a limited choice of pitch materials at any one time that has remained with him ever since.[6] But they also suggest an ambivalence towards highly restrictive 'pre-compositional' systems which was to be only temporarily eclipsed by his encounters with Darmstadt radicalism.

Dallapiccola was the last major figure from the previous generation whom Berio felt compelled to 'exorcize'. He now moved on to take up the challenges posed by his own contemporaries. In retrospect, this too may seem like an exorcism: it was only in the process of weighing up what these new approaches had to offer that he began to map out the features that were to give so distinctive a turn to his work over the next decade.

II
THE FIFTIES: FROM ELECTRONIC
STUDIO TO ORCHESTRA

Berio's four-week trip to Tanglewood in 1952 also opened up more directly innovatory perspectives, for by happy coincidence he thus found himself in New York on 28 October when the first public concert in the United States to include electronic music was given at the Museum of Modern Art. Primarily devoted to instrumental music by Varèse, the programme also featured tape pieces by Otto Luening and Vladimir Ussachewsky. Ussachewsky had been a prime mover in exploring the manipulation of tape-recorded instrumental sound, and his *Sonic Contours*, a montage of taped piano sounds that had been speeded up, slowed down, reversed, etc., was the only substantial electronic piece heard in this concert (although Luening's three brief pieces derived from recorded flute sounds followed the same principles). Berio found *Sonic Contours* a rather rudimentary affair musically, but he was intrigued by the possiblities that such resources opened up, and returned to Milan determined to explore further. He was soon to have his opportunity. Dallapiccola had furnished him with a warm letter of introduction to Luigi Rognoni, then running the 'Third Programme' for the RAI, Italy's national radio and television company. Contacts within the RAI proliferated, and in 1953 he was commissioned to produce the soundtrack for a series of television films. While working on these he also tried his hand at a short tape piece, *Mimusique No. 1*, whose basic material was neither flute nor piano, but a gun shot.

The contacts that Berio made, and the projects that he started during 1953 were to mould his career for the rest of the decade. He began drafting proposals for an electronic studio to be set up at the RAI. To do this he needed to gather as much information as possible, and when a conference on electronic music was announced in Basle in the autumn of that year, he set off to explore. There he met Karlheinz Stockhausen. But his most important encounter had taken place earlier in the year, and as a result of a journey in the opposite direction. Having discovered that

Hermann Scherchen was conducting in Genoa, Berio had set off to hear the concert, and took the opportunity to introduce himself. Scherchen suggested that Berio should seek out his ex-pupil, Bruno Maderna, who even at this stage in his career was becoming a pivotal figure in European music. Maderna had been involved with the development of the Darmstadt Summer School since 1949, and was already, through his compositions and his conducting, a tireless advocate for the new directions in musical thought that were emerging from these annual encounters. When Maderna and Berio met in Milan, the rapport was immediate. They shared enthusiasms for an encyclopaedic range of music, past and present, and a cheerful scepticism in the face of the doctrinaire polemics that were rapidly growing up around the 'New Music'. Both were intensely curious about the potential of electronic resources: indeed, Maderna had already taken a first step towards exploring these in his *Musica su due dimensioni* for flute, cymbal, and tape of 1952, generally credited with being the first piece ever to combine instrumental and taped sound.

In 1954 they set their curiosity to work, collaborating to produce for the RAI what was in effect a radiophonic portrait of Milan, *Ritratto di città*. Later in the same year Maderna returned to the RAI studios to try his hand at the pioneering techniques developed by Eimert, Meyer-Eppler, and Stockhausen at Cologne in the previous year. The result, *Sequenze e Strutture*, was his first piece using purely electronic resources. Berio meanwhile was pressing ahead with his plans for a fully fledged electronic studio to such effect that by the time it opened in August 1955, Maderna had been persuaded to throw in his lot with the project as co-director, with Dr Alfredo Lietti as technical consultant, and Marino Zuccheri as the invaluable and omnipresent technical assistant.

Their new creation was baptized, somewhat curiously, the *Studio di fonologia musicale* (a fine-sounding name imposed from above by the RAI authorities, who clearly entertained a generous conception of the limits of phonology).[1] Unimpressed by the latter-day *guerre des bouffons* that was developing between Parisian *musique concrète* and the *Elektronische Musik* of Cologne, Berio and Maderna set out to incorporate the best of both into the Milan studio.

Ironically, it was one of the technical limitations of the studio that created its most individual feature. Stockhausen's search for a coherent method of timbre-synthesis relied upon the excellent re-recording facilities available at Cologne radio, which encouraged him to attempt building up each sound analytically, layer by layer. In the Milan studio sound-quality deteriorated rather more quickly with repeated re-recordings, and Berio therefore set up a bank of nine oscillators as his basic sound-source. The experience of working with complex sounds had an immediate impact upon his instrumental writing, but it was also to re-emerge many years later, and in hugely expanded form, in the experiments in subtractive synthesis that Berio pioneered at the *Institut de Recherche et Coordination Acoustique Musique* (IRCAM), in Paris.

In the autumn and winter of 1955 Berio and Maderna set to work, collaborating upon a set of studies to illustrate the potential of the studio. Each was also working on an individual project— Berio on *Mutazioni* and Maderna on *Notturno*—so that by May 1956 they were able to give their first concert of electronic music at the RAI. They now began inviting foreign composers to work in the Milan studio: Pousseur, with whom Berio had formed an enduring friendship after their encounter at Darmstadt in the summer of 1956, came in the following year to work on *Scambi*, a work that entered into the spirit of Berio's fascination with complex sound by using filtered white noise; and in 1958 Cage spent four months working on *Fontana Mix*. But their entrepreneurial activities extended well beyond the electronic studio. In 1956 they began organizing a concert series devoted primarily to twentieth-century music called *Incontri Musicali*, of which the first series ran in Milan the following year, and the second in 1958 in Naples with the support of the RAI. Berio set about editing a journal of the same name, of which four numbers were to appear between 1956 and 1959. Maderna meanwhile persuaded Ghedini to allow him to give a course on serial music at the Conservatorio, which ran from 1957 to 1958.

This was not an isolated outburst of activity. Challenges to long-established habit were to be heard and seen on all sides: the Piccolo Teatro was coming to turbulent life under the direction of Giorgio Strehler (with whom Maderna collaborated in a famous production of Brecht's *Threepenny Opera*); Milanese galleries were beginning to take a predominant role in the marketing of contemporary art. Indeed, the very skyline of Milan was sprouting new and challenging shapes as the Olivetti offices (1956),the Torre Velasca (1957), the Torre Pirelli (1958–9) and the Torre

Galfa (1959) rose from the ground. Berio and Maderna were providing the musical complement to one of Milan's most adventurous decades.

Berio's own work in the *Studio di fonologia* during 1957 moved beyond the exploratory stage, and began to open up new territory. In *Perspectives* he limited his resources to four types of electronic sound, one of which was particularly important in establishing the work's character. He recorded sine waves of differing pitch, cut the tapes into small pieces, and made of them a *montage* with a regularly recurring pattern. Played at their original recording speed, these produced a sort of manic tintinnabulation, such as can be heard at the start of the piece. But speeded up, the individual components merged to produce a single complex sound with a characteristically shimmering quality. Berio had, in other words, found a means of generating complex timbre by accelerating micro-montages: a stimulating and relatively rapid alternative to the painstaking superposition of basic components pioneered by Stockhausen a few years earlier.

The experience of *Perspectives* spilled over into his next two projects. The first of these, *Thema (Omaggio a Joyce)* (1958) was the culmination of an investigation, with Umberto Eco, into the musical aspects of language. Its links with Berio's subsequent works for voice are so strong that it is best discussed alongside them in Chapter V. The second was *Différences*, written during 1958–9 for Boulez's *Domaine Musicale* concert series. *Différences* was Berio's response to a problem that was also exercising some of his closest associates: that of using electronic resources side by side with traditional instruments. Work in the studio entailed not only (perhaps not even primarily) a search for 'new sounds', but also new ways of thinking about musical material. To take only the most obvious issue, the primacy of pitch as a primary focus for structure was severely challenged. If instead comparative densities of texture and qualities of timbre were to be used as vehicles for structure, a new sense of large-scale formal priorities might also have to be developed.

Even in 1952, Maderna had acknowledged the tension between what were potentially different modes of musical thought in the title of his *Musica su due dimensioni*. At that juncture the resources at his disposal were somewhat rudimentary, but by 1958 he was in a position to realize a complex and extended dialogue between flute and tape, and although using fresh materials, he chose to retain the same title. Pousseur then set about confronting the problem on a more ambitious scale in *Rimes* (1958–9) which, as the title implies, sought out 'rhymes' between three orchestral groups and electronic sound-sources. But Berio's concern was not with setting up a dialogue between two dimensions, each with its own priorities, but with establishing a continuum between them, thus allowing him to think in terms of large-scale processes, rather than momentary interactions. So, while writing for a live chamber ensemble of flute, clarinet, harp, viola, and cello, he recorded the same instruments on tape, and submitted these to an increasingly radical succession of transformations. Taking the maximum identity of instruments and tape as the point of departure and return in each section, he then structured the piece around five different phases of electronic transformation, the more extreme of which rendered their original sources quite unrecognizable (a process paralleled by the pitch organization which departs from and returns to a pivotal D). This ebb and flow between natural and transformed sound was the harbinger of his work during the seventies and eighties on real-time transformation of instrumental sound discussed in Chapter VI. It also anticipated one of the hallmarks of his large-scale work: a pleasure in mapping out a field of compositional possibilities between poles that may at first glance seem distant, even incompatible (in the knowledge, fostered by a generation of structuralist critics, that on a formal level human praxes are united by a labyrinth of analogies). In *Différences* the distance is not yet that great, but Berio's appetite for setting up a fruitful contradiction within which to work is already in evidence.

In one respect, *Différences* set the seal on a process of cross-fertilization that had been developing within Berio's music over several years. Side by side with his explorations into unknown territory in the studio, he had been testing himself against previous generations by an intensive cultivation of the orchestra. But the series of major works from *Nones* (1954) to *Epifanie* (1959–61) that established his European reputation show an evolution in the handling of orchestral sound that was in part determined by his experiences in the electronic studio. Two aspects of his work there made a particular contribution to this evolution: the experience of counterpointing complex layers of sound, and the gestural style of writing that provided rhetorical continuity in the absence of more traditional harmonic frames of reference. (Indeed, the almost aggressive physicality of his approach to a medium that had in effect abolished the human body reached its apogee in *Momenti* for four-track tape (1960), the last purely electronic work that Berio was to produce.)

The technical framework within which Berio could begin to plan such large-scale instrumental works was locked into place in 1953 by his encounter with Maderna. In that year Maderna was beginning to incorporate into his own compositions the revolutionary change of technical perspective that had swept through the Darmstadt summer courses in 1951 and 1952. The extension of serial thought to cover all aspects of sound—rhythm, dynamics, timbre as well as pitch—was a phenomenon that Berio approached with a characteristic mixture of curiosity and caution. But such was his flair for rapid assimilation that by 1954 he was already putting these techniques to use in planning his first major orchestral work, *Nones*. 1954 also saw his first trip to Darmstadt, but it was when he returned in 1956 that he made a distinctive mark there, with performances of *Cinque Variazioni* and *Nones*, to which Maderna devoted an analytical discussion.

Nones had originally been planned as a secular oratorio based upon W. H. Auden's poem of the same name (one of a series reinterpreting for a disenchanted world the canonical hours). But the poem was a long one, and any complete setting would have been a daunting task: so Berio finally contented himself with linking five orchestral sections from the projected work to form an autonomous piece. He thus returned to the free variation form—a series of sections all elaborating upon the same basic material—that sustained him throughout this period of experiment from the mainly pre-serial *Cinque variazioni* (1953) discussed in Chapter I, through the *Variazioni* for chamber orchestra (1953–4) and *Nones* itself, to *Allelujah I* (1955), which had already moved beyond linear pitch serialization. The high seriousness of Darmstadt as transmitted by Maderna seems to have activated Berio's iconoclast streak, for *Nones* is based upon a thirteen-note series, albeit one of impeccable internal symmetries. The series, set out in Ex. II.1*a*, pivots around a central A♭, with each half mirroring the other in retrograde inversion. The central pivot apart, the series breaks down into groups of three that permutate major/minor third relationships (notes 8–10 are the 'fratello' theme familiar from the *Cinque Variazioni*). Between the groups run chains of thirds such as must have raised many a neo-

Ex. II.1 Pitch Series for *Nones*

Webernian eyebrow at Darmstadt. Because of the series' internal structure, its twelve transpositions read forward and backwards exhaust its potential. Perhaps because of this, and because of the series' limited variety of interval content, Berio chose to diversify his options by the device, well known to students of Berg, of reading from either end to the centre, as in Ex. II.1*b*.

As an example of Berio's relatively free use of these resources, we may take the opening seven bars from the second section of *Nones*, transcribed in Ex. II.2. Taking Ex. II.1*a* as P_0 (for the series at this transposition is indeed used as a sort of 'tonic', a point of departure and return), then the solo violin's line employs R_7, while low strings and timps accompany with the first seven notes of Ex. II.1*b*. They in turn are answered, using the same

Ex. II.2 *Nones*, reduction of bars 40–6

rhythm, by cello, clarinets, vibraphone, and guitar subjecting P_9 to a more complex permutation. Starting from the central F, they jump to the outside notes, then to the notes in the middle of each half, from whence they work back towards the centre (with the missing Bb provided by the violin). In other words here, as in *Chamber Music*, the series provides a set of resources to be used as flexibly as the composer's imagination dictates.

His treatment of parameters other than pitch in *Nones* explored the device of 'synthetic number' that had first been expounded at Darmstadt in 1951 by Goeyvaerts when analysing his *Sonata for Two Pianos*, and taken up by Stockhausen in *Kreuzspiel*. Rather than impose serial orderings upon rhythm, dynamics, etc. and leave these to interact, Berio assigned to each of four factors— position in the pitch series, duration, intensity, and mode of playing—a numerical value. Reflecting the title of Auden's poem (for nones is the ninth hour), each combination of these had to add up to nine or more (and every unit above nine would generate a semiquaver rest).[2] As might be expected, this system was allowed to evolve as he worked through the piece, with new durational values being substituted, and so forth. Only the pitch series remained as a consistent point of reference. So that although much of the score shares with totally serialized pieces note by note changes of dynamics, attack, etc., it is in fact the result of choice within a more malleable matrix of possibilities. Again, though, there is an element of iconoclasm in Berio's use of this device. Goeyvaerts and Stockhausen had been attracted to it precisely because it balanced out the distribution of materials between parameters. Berio, on the contrary, chose to use it within a highly differentiated context. Even when conceived as an oratorio, it had been intended that *Nones* should juxtapose extremes —on the orchestral level those of density and rarification of texture, on the harmonic level, a polarization between bare octaves and maximum chromatic density.[3] It is this feature which gives the work its large-scale shape, for each of the work's five sections moves towards a moment of maximum density before giving way to the next. The rarified, *klangfarbenmelodie*-based textures that Berio otherwise draws from his orchestra show him already entirely at home in the medium, although as yet only taking his first steps towards the strikingly individual orchestral sound that was to follow.

Auden's poem also interacts with the serial underpinning of

Nones in another and more graphic way. The poem is a sustained but secular meditation on the crucifixion—on our collective willingness to kill, and on how we make sense (or refuse to make sense) of the resultant corpse. Echoing the act of violence that underpins the poem, Berio uses nervous, semidemiquaver side-drum attacks that map an irregular progress through the work. The positioning of these is, however, determined by a technical feature familiar from *Chamber Music*—the convergence of different serial lines upon common pitches.

Encouraged by the undoubted success that *Nones* had scored, Berio began work upon a more adventurous project. By now his experiments with electronic resources were habituating him to a polyphony between layers of sound. Seeking to transcribe such complex musical situations into instrumental terms, and thereby to create an 'apparent alleluiatic disorder kept at bay by hidden symmetries'[4] he decided to call his new work *Allelujah*. Although conceived for resources roughly corresponding to the conventional orchestra, Berio divided his instruments into six different groups, most of them of heterogeneous composition, set as far apart on the stage as possible. His hope was that superimposed layers of material would thus be heard to interact, but at the work's first performance in Cologne in 1957 it became clear to him that, what with the *pointilliste* style of writing and the difficulty in spacing out such a wide range of instruments, this aim was not being achieved. He therefore withdrew the work, and began a process of radical recomposition. The result was *Allelujah II* (1958), a considerably more substantial work that solved the problem of differentiation between layers by distributing its five groups of instruments around the concert hall, but that also staked out for the first time an unmistakably personal idiom.

The parallels between Berio's *Allelujah* project and Stockhausen's *Gruppen* have often been remarked upon. Both were started in 1955, and both reached first performance in their final forms in 1958. But despite such surface similarities as the distribution of instrumental groups around the concert hall, and the powerful exuberance of the writing for brass choirs, the two works stem from quite disparate preoccupations. Stockhausen was led to his polychoral solution in an attempt to find time structures that would relate logically to his organization of pitch structures. Berio had no such complex theoretical motivation—his fascination was with the aural experience of complexity as such, and the new aesthetic regions to which such overloading of sensory input led.

Although Berio withdrew *Allelujah I*, we cannot therefore ignore it, for it constitutes an essential stepping-stone in the development of his thinking about musical process and structure.[5] From his exploration of pitch-based serialism, Berio had learnt to harness the extraordinary transformational potential contained in transposing given pitches from one register to another, and reshaping rhythm and dynamics. He now felt free in *Allelujah I* to take as his starting-point not a series, but a substantive, freely composed section which, through such transformations, could generate much of the subsequent material. Although this section starts from and gravitates back to the note Bb (as does therefore the rest of the work), it is otherwise conceived as being devoid of strongly polarized elements, and to this end gradually uses up almost every note within a five octave span (the only major exception being Bb's polar opposite, E, which is only transposed over a three-octave range). The same pitch materials are then restated in two further versions, though transformed beyond recognition by modifications in other parameters. These three sections then provide the materials for a further three. In the first of these, the second half of section two is superimposed on the first half retrograded. In the second and third, the same principle of superimposition is applied to entire sections: all of which generates an ever more thriving 'alleluiatic disorder', as Berio intended.

When Berio returned to these materials in the summer of 1957, he reworked them quite radically. Thus the only materials from *Allelujah I* that are immediately recognizable in *Allelujah II* are the section that was the starting-point for the whole project (bars 1–25 in *Allelujah II*), the first half of section 2, albeit considerably transformed, and the closing section with its chorus of flutes and pitched percussion. Other episodes, such as the powerful and extended section for brass and percussion (bars 97–175) are already present *in nuce* in *Allelujah I*, but otherwise *Allelujah II* represents a remarkable step forward. The inner life of individual layers is now itself richly complex, but as a result differentiation between them is clear-cut. This can be best illustrated by comparing a few bars from the second section of *Allelujah I* given in reduced score in Ex. II.3 with their counterparts in *Allelujah II*, set out in Ex. II.4.

20

Ex. II.3 *Allelujah*, reduction of bars 41–5

Clearly, pitch relations in the first four bars of Ex. II.3 have been drastically rearranged in Ex. II.4—primarily by redistribution of register so as to reduce a gamut of four and a half octaves to two and a half. Thus a widely spaced, fragmentary polyphony is replaced by a relatively dense band of sound. But even more typical of the change that has taken place in Berio's conception of instrumental sound is the transformation of the clarinet line from

Ex. II.4 *Allelujah II*, reduction of bars 44–8

Ex. II.3 into the heterophonic cluster of violin lines of Ex. II.4. Indeed, the cello line that responds to the clarinet in the last bar of Ex. II.3 is transformed in Ex. II.4 into a whole new layer of sound introduced by a different group.

Allelujah II was not Berio's final experiment with multiple groups, for in the following year he began work on *Tempi concertati*, where four chamber groups dispersed about the stage, and co-ordinated by a solo flautist, recapitulated the aspirations of *Allelujah I* on a more manageable scale. But as far as the full orchestra was concerned, Berio now set his mind to reuniting the fragmented, polychoral disposition of *Allelujah II* into a single large ensemble—but one that could move between articulating counterpointed layers of sound, and functioning as a single, though often densely complex unit. So he began work on a series of short orchestral pieces, the first three of which were performed in 1960 under the title of *Quaderni I*. *Quaderni II* followed in 1961, and a further piece was combined with one from each of the previous groups to form *Quaderni III* in 1962, but all of these pieces achieved their best-known form when Berio interleaved them with a cycle of vocal settings to form *Epifanie* (1961). If Berio was to achieve differentiation between complex sound-layers within a unified orchestra, he had to rely upon homogeneity of timbre within a given layer. He provided himself with the basic materials for this by rationalizing his orchestra. Where in *Allelujah II* there had been a flute quartet, and indeed complementary horn quartets and trumpet trios placed in different groups, now in the *Quaderni* all wind families were organized in groups of four (save for six horns and a single tuba), and strings in groups of eight (save for six double-basses). Berio demanded three groups of violins, the third of which was to be placed around the back of the orchestra to act as a form of echo-chamber, allowing specific harmonic configurations that had been established in the foreground to become a background layer for others. The orchestra for the *Quaderni* was completed by a rich selection of pitched and unpitched percussion.

The *Quaderni* (literally 'Notebooks', and hereafter referred to by the letters used to designate them in *Epifanie*) are above all virtuoso studies in orchestral sound—the culmination of a decade of investigation. They show a meticulous control of nuances of harmonic density, rhythm, and timbre, but as means to an end. For here more than anywhere, Berio explored the global effects

23

of interactions between these elements. (This intensive focus upon questions of texture and density makes of the *Quaderni* a magnificent foil to the vocal settings of *Epifanie*, whose melodies appear among them as musical 'epiphanies': moments of lucidity and focus that parallel the young James Joyce's literary conception.) Thus the huge harmonic aggregates, in part chromatically saturated and covering much of the orchestral gamut, that Berio uses as staccato punctuation marks or as massive sound-blocks, demand new forms of differentiation from the ear. In part, they can be distinguished by the placing of 'windows' at different registers within the saturated blocks. But, more importantly, they emphasize the range of possibilities at work in an orchestral *tutti*. At one extreme, these aggregates are layered, so that instruments of similar timbre play adjacent notes within them. At the other, they are fully integrated by dispersing instruments of the same family on to non-adjacent notes. The more subtle variants between these two poles often lie at the very borderline of perception: particularly so when used as staccato attacks, as in the latter part of *Epifanie C*. They alternate with other ways of exploring complex musical objects that invite a greater measure of analytical listening. Aggregates may be spelt out by chains of overlapping entries (ancestors of the 'wave-form' delineation of harmonic fields discussed in Chapter IV) as from bar 19 of *Epifanie B* on. Or the aggregates may be sustained, and different dynamic contours assigned to different timbre groupings, so that a variety of harmonic formations are momentarily spotlighted within them, as in *Epifanie E*. Finally, provided that the aggregate retains a reasonable measure of internal harmonic differentiation, it may be taken as a fixed, or slowly evolving pitch field, from which each of many superposed instrumental lines constructs its own melodic shape, thus producing a magmatic tutti, as in *Epifanie G*.

These fixed pitch fields reflect an approach to harmonic thought common to both Berio and Pousseur, and given theoretical form by the latter (albeit in somewhat elliptical form) in his essay 'Outline of a Method' of 1957. Pousseur had begun work on a series of piano pieces in which he derived his pitch materials from a series of 'harmonic fields'—temporarily fixed pitch groupings characteristically dominated by one or two intervals, and the notes chromatically adjacent to them. Berio was perhaps more interested in the spirit than in the letter of Pousseur's formulations. But the opening measures of *Epifanie A* show him using a roughly

24

analogous approach as a means of maintaining harmonic control within complex textures. Within them, a series of harmonic fields consolidate and break up in fairly rapid succession, each in turn explored by a counterpoint of flutter-tongue flutes and trumpets (a favourite combination), echoed by violins.

A harmonic summary of the first sixteen bars is given in Ex. II.5. White note-heads indicate a fixed field; black note-heads are used for brief *tutti* chords, pitches extraneous to the fixed fields, and pitches introduced in the aftermath of a field or a chord, usually to fill out gaps within the previous structure. Lines between note-heads indicate chromatic saturation. All notes are shown in descending pitch order, rather than order of occurence. The fields in bars 1–3 and 7–9 certainly reflect Pousseur's approach in some measure, the first marked by the presence of augmented and perfect fourths, the second (a twelve-tone field)

Ex. II.5 Pitch fields from *Epifanie A*

by the strong influence of chains of minor thirds. They also share a common nucleus, indicated by the curved bracket. Similarly, both the upper part of the chord at bar 13, and the field at bars 15–16 can be variously derived by transposing elements of the field at bars 7–9 up a semitone (the latter relationship indicated by the square bracket). Consequently, the ear always percieves a gap of a fourth or augmented fourth maintained in the middle of the treble clef as these aggregates form and dissolve.

Such transitory use of fixed fields was to remain characteristic of Berio's music until he began to explore their potential for the generation of extensive melodic structures in the mid-sixties (see Chapter III). But fixed fields represented only one of several approaches to organizing pitches that Berio had at his disposal. Indeed, glancing through the rest of *Epifanie A* one finds that within a few pages the ever-denser texture (based upon a 'thickened out' version of bars 7–9) gives way to a more traditional approach. For from the upbeat to bar 30, three-note cells characterized by the leap of a tritone plus one of the notes contained within it begin to play a dominant role (anticipated by bars 1–3). But just as the harmonic fields of the first section gradually lost their powers of differentiation through the addition of extra notes, so too this quasi-motivic material loses its identity as it is subjected to increasing transformation, and from bar 93 the original timbre resources return, abetted by flutter-tongue horns and trombones, pitched percussion, and full strings. Now, however, they operate without the discipline of a fixed field, and instead agglomerate into a series of wandering, chromatically saturated, pitch clouds within which all harmonic or motivic differentiation is annulled. (This gesture, too, is anticipated in the opening bars: a polyphony of voices moving upward through the chromatically saturated lower portion of the field used in bars 10–12 gives a foretaste of what is to come.)

It is characteristic of Berio's orchestral textures that each line within the counterpoint of voices exploring a fixed field makes its own musical sense. The orchestral player is not asked to contribute a few grains of material to a whole that only takes on coherence when heard globally. This tension between an often impossible abundance of individual musical gestures continues Berio's search for an 'alleluiatic' style of writing not dissimilar in effect (nor perhaps in intention) to the calculated superabundance of some fifteenth-century polyphony. Although Berio's insistence upon the special state triggered by bombarding perception with a richer range of stimuli than it can fully cope with carries no metaphysical implications, it challenges the narrowly focused and controlled mode of attention which the adult individual in our culture is encouraged to identify with 'self'-preservation. Certainly, it is an arena to which Berio has chosen to return time and again, constructing perceptual labyrinths that will include not just notes, but words and, in due course, theatre.

In bringing together the instrumental and vocal pieces that make up *Epifanie*, Berio suggested nine different sequences in which they might be played, based on relationships of harmonic or textural congruence—he described them as 'alliterations' —between the end of one piece and the beginning of the next.[6] In practice he has shown a marked preference for the first of these, and it is significant that this should be the one that marks a clear progression within the texts of the vocal cycle, moving from Proustian aestheticism to Brecht's blunt interrogation of the ethics of artistic activity. No doubt Berio's *hommage* to the malleable forms espoused by Boulez during this period was sincere enough, but his commanding sense of large-scale dramatic structure was such that he did not choose to repeat the experiment. More significant from the point of view of Berio's future practice was the simple act of devising a framework within which these diversely oriented cycles could coexist. Berio's creative concerns were already beginning to diversify. As they became more disparate, and centrifugal, so the periodic compulsion to recreate some central ground by activating a synthesis betwen them became stronger. From now on, all of Berio's major works were to bear the stamp of this tension.

III

MELODY AND HARMONY

In 1960, Berio returned to the Summer School at Tanglewood to teach composition. With him went Cathy Berberian, who made her American début with the first performance of *Circles*. This journey back to the place where he had completed his own apprenticeship was also a prophetic one. Within three years Berio was to have transferred the focus of his activities to the United States, there to remain until 1971. And for the rest of the decade he was to support himself primarily through the teaching of composition. By now the increasing attention being given to his work in Europe and the United States was opening up a range of opportunities that were not easily combined with his job at the RAI, and accordingly, having completed his work on *Visage* (see Chapter V), in 1961 he resigned from the *Studio di fonologia*. For the next two years he remained based in Milan, but already he was beginning to adopt the life of constant travel that he was to maintain with such vigour over the next fifteen years.

In the summer of 1961, he taught at the Dartington Summer School, and returned the following summer. But the spring of 1962 offered an opportunity with more far-reaching consequences. Darius Milhaud, who had followed Berio's recent work with keen interest, and who had since 1947 combined teaching at Mills College, Oakland, California with a professorship at the Paris Conservatoire, asked Berio to teach the spring semester at Mills College while he was in Paris. The arrangement worked well, and since Milhaud wanted to spend the whole of the 1963–64 academic year in Paris, he asked Berio to take his place.

On his first trip to Mills College, Berio had met a gifted young student of psychology, Susan Oyama. On his return, the relationship flourished: by 1964 they were living together, in 1965 they were married. But this did not destroy the remarkable working relationship that Berio and Cathy Berberian had built up: in 1964 he wrote *Folk Songs* for her, and in 1965 began work on the piece that more than any other was tailored to her extraordinary gifts: *Sequenza III*. In the autumn of 1964, Oyama began her doctoral research at Harvard University, where Berio also took on a semester's teaching. In December of that year he then went to Berlin with a grant from the Ford Foundation, but spent only sporadic amounts of time there, since he was regularly commuting to Paris, where the first performance of *Laborintus II* was being prepared.

In the autumn of 1965, Berio took up the post at the Juilliard School of Music in New York that he was to occupy for the next six years. Since Oyama was still pursuing her research at Harvard, Berio at first commuted between Boston (where their daughter Marina was born in 1966) and New York. Soon, however, the family were able to settle in Hoboken, New Jersey: their son, Stefano, was born there in 1968. Berio's work at the Juilliard School was not confined to teaching composition and analysis: he also founded the Juilliard Ensemble in order to promote the performance of contemporary music. Yet although the official record of these years seems to spell out a life of academic calm, a good deal of his time was in fact spent in hotels as he flew from one musical centre to the next fostering the rapid growth in popularity of his music. Although the 'international' composer is no new phenomenon, and Berio's constant travels during the sixties and early seventies are merely those of many a previous generation of Italian composers writ large, the lack of roots within any given cultural milieu certainly served to entrench his 'omnivorous' curiosity and openness.

Some commentators have been tempted to suggest a relationship between the direct, vivid idiom that Berio was consolidating during his years in the United States, and his encounter with American culture.[1] Admittedly, certain aspects of an American tradition of experimental theatre find their way into *Esposizione* (1962–3, subsequently withdrawn), or *Opera* (1969–70), and *Questo vuol dire che* (1968–9) might be viewed as a well-organized 'happening'. But there is little in Berio's purely musical style during this period that does not have roots in his work in Milan during the late fifties and early sixties: the United States was for him a work-place, not a source for further 'exorcisms'.

But his work from the sixties does show a stable, and highly individual musical language, many of whose features have remained permanent resources. It will make for greater clarity to outline the development of each of these separately, rather than attempt to account for his formidable output through the sixties and seventies on a chronological basis. This can be done all the more readily since with the completion of the *Quaderni* Berio shifted his creative focus. Having explored orchestral and electronic resources at some length, he now began to concentrate upon the solo performer, and the human voice. Taking up the example of his 1958 *Sequenza* for solo flute, he produced a series of further *Sequenzas*, each for a solo performer. By now, this has become his most long-standing project, the most recent additions being *Sequenza X* for trumpet (1984), and *Sequenza XI* for guitar (1987–8). Although this was a spontaneous choice, it had happy consequences for the more general dissemination of his music. Demanding orchestral works such as *Allelujah II* or the *Quaderni* required a great deal of rehearsal time, and were consequently not heard as often as they merited, whereas such virtuoso performers as Berberian, Gazzelloni, and Dempster were happy to repeat the immediately popular *Circles* and *Sequenzas I, III*, and *V* wherever they went. Berio's treatment of the human voice is highly distinctive, and warrants a separate chapter, so the vocal and dramatic works of the sixties will be discussed here only in as much as they illustrate some of the technical aspects of his musical language.

Concentrating upon solo instruments and upon the human voice entailed thinking in terms of sustained melodic structures. Berio's serial and pre-serial experiences had already provided him with resources that were particularly adapted to the task. A closer look at the flute *Sequenza* will help to illustrate two of them. Serial thinking had sensitized a whole generation of composers to an exhaustive use of the chromatic spectrum, and to the distinctive melodic potential of sevenths, ninths, and their transposed equivalents. Berio had already found a method of satisfying these concerns independently of any serial ordering in the *Cinque Variazioni* of 1952–3, where he based his materials upon transpositions from a meandering chromatic ascent or descent (see Ex. I.3). He took up this device once more in the *Sequenza*, whose opening line is set out in Ex. III.1. The darting agility that characterizes much of the work is strongly conditioned by it, and Berio manifestly enjoys the *tour de force* required to generate a constantly changing line from so simple, and so constantly recurring an underlying process. Extended examples will be found on page 2, lines 5–6 and page 4, from the end of line 3 to the first Bb of line 5 in the score.[2]

Ex. III.1 *Sequenza* for flute, p. 1, system 1

Ex. III.2 *Sequenza* for flute, p. 1, system 3

Ex. III.3 *Sequenza* for flute, p. 5, systems 4–6

Sequenza I also creates a linear equivalent to the procedure explored in *Allelujah I*. It, too, takes an extensive passage of music, and reinterpets its pitch patterns by all the changes of register and rhythmic profile that serialism had made so central to the composer's work. This occurs once towards the middle of the

31

piece (from page 2, line 9 of the score) and a second time at the end. Ex. III.2 reproduces lines 3 and 4 of page 1. If one compares Exx. III.1 and III.2 with Ex. III.3, which reproduces the equivalent material from the final page (since Berio omits the materials of page 1, line 2 in this final version), the extent of the transformation will be clear.

In reworking his materials in *Sequenza I*, Berio added or subtracted individual pitches to the sequence from time to time, or else permutated the order of pitches. These devices came to the fore in his vocal music of the early sixties, where the potential for reworking melodic shapes by registral transposition was perforce limited. They reached a point of classic elegance and simplicity in the Proust setting from *Epifanie*. Here Berio established a simple tripartite structure: an initial melodic statement followed, at bar 12, by a section in which a five-note group gains one extra note in each of three repetitions before generating a climax. The initial melodic structure then returns at bar 17, its internal

Ex. III.4 *Epifanie a*, vocal line only, *a* bars 2–7 and *b* 17–21

relationships quietly but consistently reworked. Ex. III.4 compares the start of the melody (a) with its reprise (b).

A similar procedure is made visually explicit in the score of 'Stazione II' from *Passaggio* (1962). Here each section of the vocal line is repeated, and note-tails in opposite directions indicate which pitches are to be sung the first time and which the second. As in the Proust setting, the vocal line is conceived as an autonomous structure; Berio therefore provides a quiet, semi-independent background layer of instrumental sound. This way of creating an expansive, but varied vocal line has become a permanent resource in Berio's work: other notable examples are *Calmo* (1974), and *Il Ricordo*, with which Berio concludes both Part I and Part II of *La vera storia* (1977–81).[3]

In most of these instances, the significance of individual pitches within a sequence is altered, often radically, by reworking rhythm. Berio's working notes may well contain a repertoire of rhythmic gestures, but approaching rhythm as a fixed sequence analogous to pitch is less common in his work. One important exception is *O King*, composed in 1967 as a memorial to Martin Luther King whose name, pieced together from its component phonemes, provides a text for the vocal line (a process discussed further in Chapter V). That line is generated from a cycle in which seven pitches each occur thrice in different configurations. The repetitions of this twenty-one-unit pitch cycle interact with those of a rhythmic cycle of twenty units (though this is not as strictly maintained as is the pitch cycle). This process naturally inflects the melodic shape differently at each cycle—the more so as strongly differentiated durations in the rhythmic cycle bring new notes to the fore each time round.

In effect, this procedure amounts to the cyclic permutation of a fixed pitch field, whose harmonic implications are realized by a constantly shifting pattern of echoes and anticipations from the instrumental ensemble. As might therefore be expected, the chromatic complement to the seven melodic pitches is also disposed as a fixed field—though of isolated notes spread over four octaves, so as to provide a contrasting background to the central melodic process. At first each of these remains at its original register, but gradually some of them begin to aquire greater mobility and appear at other octaves as well. This is the simplest of several ways in which a fixed pitch field can be made to yield a sense of process.[4]

The use of large-scale harmonic process to give shape to a work became increasingly important to Berio from the late sixties on, for it allowed him to replace the consecutive episodes from which a number of his earlier works had been built by a broad harmonic perspective that would contain, and give a wider significance to, heterogeneous surface detail. A foretaste of this approach was provided by *Sequenza V* for trombone (1966). In the first section leading up to the point where the trombonist interjects a spoken 'Why?',[5] the trombone gradually brings into play, one after another, the notes of a fixed dodecaphonic field, and is thus able to build its melodic line from an expanding range of resources.

In *Sequenza V* this process governs only a single section, but in *Sequenza VII* for oboe (1969) it is extended by a gradual introduction of octave transposition so as to provide a backbone for the entire work. *Sequenza VII* pivots around its first note, a B,[6] which is sounded quietly in the background by another instrument for the rest of the performance. The oboe quickly establishes a highly structured pitch field, whose dominance then gradually dissolves as more and more of the chromatic gamut becomes available. Because the score is set within a durational framework that repeats identically from line to line, a summary of this process can be made simply by recording what new pitches are introduced into the melody from one line to the next. This is set out in Ex. III.5: the first introduction of a pitch class is shown by a white note-head, and the introduction of subsequent transpositions by black note-heads.

Ex. III.5 Outline pitch structure of *Sequenza VII*

By the end of the piece, the oboe has explored its complete chromatic gamut up to a top G, save for the five notes bracketed on a separate stave. Their absence is by no means accidental. The two Bs must be excluded in order to underline the centrality of the opening note. The other three absent notes ensure that the characteristics of the original fixed field are never quite lost. In line 2, the oboe establishes a near-symmetrical structure around the opening B. But the upper and lower wings of this field are to evolve in different ways. The upper wing fills out over the next two lines into an area of relative chromatic mobility bounded by the upper Db and the F of line 4. The only pitches missing from this semi-chromatic cluster of available notes are the B discussed above, and G, a pitch class being reserved for a special role. The absence of the upper D throughout the piece thus serves as a reminder of this original boundary.

By contrast, the lower wing remains highly differentiated. The absent low B and C ensure that the bottom Bb remains an isolated point of reference. Similarly, although the low D of line 2 is joined by its neighbours E and Eb in lines 4 and 5, the gap between E and the focal B is only bridged in line 9, and not effectively filled until line 11: the absent F serves to underline this long-standing feature of the work's pitch structure. However, the corresponding gap between the focal B and the F above it is filled relatively quickly, in lines 7 and 8. (The bracketed C in line 3 serves only as the final destination of a glissando, but does not become an autonomous participant in the melodic process until line 8.) In line 9, the role of Db in defining the upper limit of the melodic gamut is finally superceded by an E. This paves the way for the one pitch class that has so far not been heard at all: a high G reserved to assume this climactic role.

Such strategic considerations, while generating a melodic process, also imply a harmonic one (the more so since in the later stages of the *Sequenza*, where much of the oboe's gamut has become available, Berio continues to use only a fairly restricted range of pitches at any given point). When in due course he came to write *Chemins IV* (1974–5) around *Sequenza VII* (a process discussed further in Chapter IV), he was able to convert harmonic implication into aural reality. Traces of this approach can be found as far back as *Nones* (for instance bars 243–73), but from *O King* onwards, the articulation of a large-scale melodic/harmonic process by a central line which throws off a constantly evolving cloud of harmonic formations around it became a dominant feature of his work. Further examples will be discussed in Chapter IV. Indeed, even so recent a work as *Requies*, written 1984–5 in memory of Cathy Berberian, is unified by this procedure.

The perception of harmony as an evolving process can only come about if the ear can clearly distinguish different types of harmonic material—and that in turn demands a wide harmonic palette. Berio's approach to establishing that range was a distinctive one. Like any other composer of his generation, he was compelled to find his own path through the ironies of post-tonal harmony, where a vast range of choice (limited only by the continuing dominance of a twelve-note scale) is regulated by relatively weak syntactic restraints: voice-leading, which in a chromatic context tends to resolve into semitonal side-steps, and nuances of relative dissonance/consonance, which rapidly lose their differentiating power within a complex harmonic context. Berio's solution was in part a reaction to the rather narrow range of seventh-and ninth-based harmonies within which the experiments in musical thought of the fifties had been carried out. He increasingly began to explore that extraordinarily rich sector of the new harmonic spectrum in which chains of thirds (and sometimes fourths) provide the ear with stepping-stones into a complex harmonic formation. Such a tendency was already apparent in the harmonic fields from *Epifanie* set out in Ex. II.5, but during the sixties it was to become a good deal more explicit. By electing to work within a harmonic range that offered such a rich gamut of possibilities, and demanded such a careful ear for individual harmonic nuance, Berio was now displaying much the same delight in mastering abundance that he had earlier shown in his approach to orchestral instrumentation. But he was also entering into a dialogue with the family ghosts that many of his contemporaries had thought politic to avoid.

The rapid evolution of his harmonic language may be gauged by comparing Ex. III.6, a short score transcription of the first bars of 'Stazione III' from *Passaggio* (1962), with the transcription from *Allelujah II* (1957–8) given in Ex. II.4. Both examples bring into play the full range of chromatic pitch classes within a few bars, yet the effect is markedly different. In Ex. II.4 linear and gestural considerations prevail against a fluid, but somewhat undifferentiated harmonic backdrop. In Ex. III.6, Berio allows himself sparer textures, but a more strongly differentiated range

of harmonies. The initial open fifth expands into a downward exploration of a third-based chord that carries no tonal connotations, but resolves in bar 7 into a chord that can for a moment be so heard (A♭ minor as supertonic of a G♭ major suggested by viola and harp) before being dissolved by the harp's low C.

Such moments of fugitive recognition are frequent in Berio's music. He never assumes that the mind exploring his music is a *tabula rasa*. By now almost all harmonic formations are loaded with connotations (even the post-Webernian grisaille that was supposed to wipe the slate clean). Berio's art lies in allowing for this ebb and flow of associations without letting it become a motive force in his harmonic thought (as has tended to be the case with a younger generation of composers). He presumes a working knowledge of the European tradition, but militates against nostalgia. This involves a delicate harmonic balancing act. Ex. III.7 gives, in short score, a simple example: the final bars from 'Stazione V' of

Passaggio. Clearly, bars 1 and 4 of Ex. III.7 are each capable of awakening tonal echoes: but they are the contradictory ones of C♯ minor and G major (and unlike the previous example are so notated). This is particularly striking in bar 4, where the open fifth at the bottom of the chord provokes strong associations, kept in place by woodwind and brass interjecting with the same chord a semitone higher. (This saturates the chromatic spectrum save for B, which is again the missing pitch when, in bar 8, instruments combine and add to the two final chords of the voices.)

The extraordinary range of nuance that could be achieved by shifting a note here or there within these complex chords (usually of at least six notes) became the focus of *Sequenza IV* for piano (1965–6)—like many of the other *Sequenzas*, as much an *étude* in a particular compositional problem as it is in particular instrumental techniques. Ex. III.8*a* reproduces the first two bars of the *Sequenza*, Ex. III.8*b* the final three bars of its first page. (The notes in brackets in III.8*b* are held by the third pedal, which throughout provides a background layer of slowly moving chords.)

Clearly, the second chord of III.8*a* has already started its metamorphoses by the final chord of III.8*b*, as has the final chord of III.8*a* in the first articulated chord of III.8*b*. The second and fourth chords of III.8*b* are part of an extensive process of transformation that has already begun. Ex. III.9 charts the progress of this chord as it reappears, transformed, at various points in the work.

There is no systematic process at work here, simply attentive experiment with the changes in nuance that come from altering different notes. Similarly, no syntactic rule governs the sequences

Ex. III.8 *Sequenza IV*, bars 1–2 and 13–15

Ex. III.9 Chord transformation in *Sequenza IV*

in which this and the various other chords subject to these processes appear and reappear save for the global procedure already familiar from *Sequenza I*, whereby extensive sections are taken up and reworked (cf. Ex. III.1–3).

One other entirely characteristic feature of Berio's style from the late fifties through to the early seventies must be mentioned, even though it cannot easily be analysed, and that is the graphically 'gestural' style of his writing. (Again, reference back to Ex. III.1–3 provides an excellent example.) Thinking in terms of discrete, vivid gestural units tends to make for a fluid and intuitive approach to rhythm, devolving any 'pre-compositional' organisation of sets or processes back into the traditional area of pitch. By the same token, the wide range of timbre, texture, and attack that Berio tends to deploy, particularly within the solo works, is used almost exclusively in the service of making the individual gesture more vivid, rather than underlining the reworking of pitch sequences, or the unfolding of pitch processes. Indeed, such works as *Sequenza II* for harp (1963) or *Sincronie* for string quartet (1964) seem to owe their cohesion almost entirely to the sustained inventiveness of their individual gestures.

The question of why one gesture might be 'more vivid' than another was one to which Berio had himself given some thought. In an essay written in 1963,[7] he was at pains to emphasize that he thought of gesture not as a spontaneous event somewhat after the manner of, say, 'action painting', but as an act significant to us because it has behind it a history. This does not, however, mean that it is to be viewed as an item in a pre-established code:

we can reach the point where we use gesture for *what it may eventually become*, thus resisting the 'natural' tendency of languages to codify, to crystallize into symbols, to transform itself into a 'catalogue of gestures', fragments of a still life . . .

This in turn means that
to be creative, gesture must be capable of destroying something, it must be dialectic and must not deprive itself of its 'theatre', even at the cost of dirtying itself—as E. Sanguineti would say—in the mud, the *palus putredinis* of experience. Which is to say that it must always contain something of what it proposes to move beyond.

IV
COMMENTARY TECHNIQUES

Although reviewing various of the components of Berio's musical language in isolation makes for clarity, it is also simplistic, for the richness of his musical thought lies precisely in his ability to combine and balance them so as to create a total structure. To show this, we must look in detail at an individual work. The choice falls on *Sequenza VI* for viola (1967) for several reasons. Firstly, because it is one of the most powerful pieces that Berio wrote during the sixties. Secondly, because it was to serve as the nucleus for a series of further works, called *Chemins*, that were built around it, adding further layers to its pre-established structure. This process was in turn to shape a good deal of Berio's work during the seventies and beyond.

The *Chemins* series had started earlier in the decade. In 1962, attracted by the evident affinity that Berio had shown for the harp in *Circles* (1960), Heinrich Strobel commissioned a concerto for harp and orchestra for Francis Pierre to play at the Donaueschingen festival. By way of focusing his thoughts, Berio first wrote a piece for solo harp, and recognizing its affinity with the *Sequenza* for flute of 1958, called it *Sequenza II*. But he then realized that *Sequenza II* could itself serve as the core of a work for harp and orchestra simply by allowing the orchestral material to proliferate from the original harp line. Only at two points in the resultant *Chemins* (literally 'paths', and so called to emphasize the pro-liferating orchestral lines) did he feel the need to interrupt the harp line, and give the orchestra its head: otherwise, he simply added extra layers on top of the pre-existent core (a procedure facilitated by the layered approach to orchestral writing discussed in Chapter II).

By the violence of its writing, *Sequenza II* had deliberately challenged conventional notions of the harp's expressive range. *Sequenza VI* performs the same office for the viola. The con-centrated aggression of its first pages sweeps aside any pre-formed notions of the viola as an instrument of melancholic introspection. Indeed, from its first harsh tremolando chord, the instrument is embroiled in a formidable task: the articulation of a serpentine counterpoint of at least four parts. The top line provides an anchor for the ear, moving inexorably upward in a chromatic progress from A to the Eb an octave and a half above. Beneath it, other lines map out a more meandering ascent—an explicit realization of the sort of wandering chromatic line that was concealed by octave transposition in Exx. I.3 or III.1. Although a four-part texture is implicit throughout (and will be made explicit in *Chemins II*), one line may leap to take over a pitch area previously occupied by another, or to start colonization of a vacant pitch area. Berio is thus able to maintain a constant variation in harmonic texture, and to generate a highly flexible counterpoint in which certain pitch processes have an enduring presence, while others prove to be evanescent. These side-stepping inner parts create a succession of harmonic variants beneath each successive pitch of the upper part's ascent. Each new chord is heralded by a new attack, and often by an introductory flurry of hemidemisemiquavers as well. Although the ferocious *fff sempre* tremolando with which the viola attacks these opening pages makes it possible to sound four-part chords, some mitigation of this overwhelming sonority is essential for both player and listeners. So individual lines may make only an intermittent appearence, etched in from time to time.

Ex. IV.1 *Sequenza VI*, p. 1, end of system 3, start of system 4

Ex. IV.1 shows an example of the resulting texture just as the ascent starts, with the upper part moving from Bb to C. Clearly, the ear is constantly invited to contrast and compare. The harmonic variants that were scattered through the score of *Sequenza IV* (see Ex. III.9) are here made explicit by direct juxtaposition. But despite the physical limitations imposed by fingering, Berio hardly ever allows the same chord structure to appear twice. He is thus able to generate an extremely rich sequence of material that can subsequently be reworked several times. But once more, a process which constituted a *tour de force* of disguise in *Sequenza I* is here made plain. The last of several such reworkings dissolves harmony into melody, whereupon a new organizational principle, the fixed pitch field, takes over—at first used as a reservoir for melodic writing, but after a final outburst of hysteria, returning to harmonic exploration of a calmer kind.

An outline of these pitch materials and processes is given in Ex. IV.2. Since the score is notated without bar-lines or rehearsal letters, reference to it is made by page number, followed by system number. (Some systems divide so as to present alternatives: these are counted as one.) Up to the end of page 4, white note-heads map the successive ascents (and one descent) of the basic material discussed above; black note-heads map ancillary materials. From page 5 on, white note-heads map fixed points of pitch reference, whether harmonic fields, or fixed chord dispositions.

Even at first glance, the crucial role played by tritones is evident. As has already been noted, the first four pages are dominated by the polarity between A and E♭. After the initial ascent from 1.1. to 2.1., answered at its climax by fierce glissando four-part chords (the first of which, with its triad-plus-semitone formation, is a cousin to the opening chord), the top line makes a more rapid descent (2.3.–2.6.). When it reaches the lower E♭, it leaps back to A, and starts another ascent (2.6.). This, however, is broken off before it encounters the lower E♭, instead skipping up in minor thirds from D (3.1.). A third ascent is attempted at 3.2., but this too peters out having got as far as E, before sinking back to E♭. After these two abortive attempts, a full ascent is made at 3.5.–3.8. which, prompted by the example of 2.6.–3.1., skips over the intervening E♭ and A.

At 3.10. there is a first intimation of the alternative process that is to take over the work. A ten-pitch fixed field, spelt out so as to emphasize the tritonal relations within it, is juggled at 4.1. into an eight-pitch field built entirely of tritones (of which the topmost is the familiar D♯-A) and then momentarily into a six-pitch field. It provides a preluding gesture leading into the final, melodic statement of the ascending process (4.2.–4.8.). This halts on its

44

penultimate note (D), and stabilizes on an F/E♭ alternation, followed by a pause.

This pause marks the transition from reworking a complex 'text' governed by process and pitch polarity to a final section governed by fixed pitch fields, and fixed harmonic 'objects'. The

Ex. IV.2 Outline pitch structure of *Sequenza VI*

Ex. IV.2 (*cont.*):

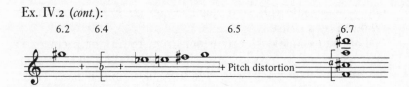

first fixed field (5.1.–5.5.), which generates a further passage of extended melodic writing, has a strong tritonal content, marked in Ex. IV.2 by square brackets. (Again, the uppermost tritone is Eb-A.) At 5.5. this field is infiltrated by a six pitch field whose four upper notes transpose down a semitone four of its own (marked by dotted lines). In 5.6. this latter takes over, proving to be a preparation for a persistently repeated chord, here labelled I.

(It is worth pausing at this point to take note of the care with which Berio prepares such harmonic focal points. Of the four pitch classes used in chord I, two—C and F♯—have been in use since the start of this section. But the other two—G and B—were rigorously excluded from the fixed field of 5.1.–5.4. The only other pitch class thus excluded, C♯,[1] is reserved to provide the basis for a second focal chord, labelled II in Ex. IV.2, where it combines with G and B, along with the relatively omnipresent Eb. Such examples of generating large-scale structure through allocating specific roles to individual pitch classes could be multiplied *ad infinitum* in Berio's work.)[2]

Chord I is challenged in 5.8. by chord II, which has been generated from it. Two pitches have risen a semitone, two a major third. A single chord at the end of 5.7. mediates between them. For a while there is battle between them, but in the latter half of 5.9. the stability of chord I is undermined by contrapuntal side-stepping reminiscent of the opening section. By 5.10., chord II has established itself as a fixed configuration to be used in parallel motion and, after one or two further chromatic brutalities inflicted on chord I, takes over entirely.

For this purpose, Berio uses either the three upper notes of this fixed configuration (indicated by vertical bracket a) or the whole chord (indicated by vertical bracket b). At 6.1. he uses the former to establish a fixed field consisting of two groups of three chromatically adjacent chords separated by a leap of a minor third. The existence of this gap is emphasized by glissandos across it. From 6.4. the full chord is used, and the gamut extended downward to the original position of chord II. From 6.5. glissandos give way to random distortions within the tremolando chords. This incipient anarchy is countered by emphasizing one of the properties of the chord. Since its upper three notes are separated by two minor sixths, any leap of a minor sixth will produce two pitch identities, and any leap of a fifth or even augmented fourth audible voice leading: a process that finally resolves on to a new chord (6.7.) whose lower three notes are separated by minor sixths.

Everything now dissolves into harmonics (6.8.). It is finally brought back down to earth by the same sequence of minor thirds that had been used to provide the 'skips' in 3.5.–3.8., and comes to rest on chord I. This ushers in the final fixed field. It is the same as that briefly used at 4.1., save that the low C has been 'used up' by chord I, and a high F has been added (a last echo from the previous section). A G♯ has also been added so that the fixed field now englobes the opening chord. The harmonic content of the field is explored in a series of quiet dyads, emphasizing its capacity to form tritones beneath open strings.

In that it is integrated by an evolving network of pitch relationships, *Sequenza VI* is typical of Berio's large-scale structural thought. But in the first part this integration is reinforced by multiple reworkings of the 'text' established by the initial ascent. All of these involve a measure of compression, and thereby extract new relationships from the 'text'. (We shall see Berio applying a similar procedure to verbal texts in the next chapter.) Ex. IV.3 shows the version of Ex. IV.1 that is heard at 3.6. Here, the second and third chords beneath B are used merely as grace notes: the second to emphasize the low E, and the third to

Ex. IV.3 *Sequenza VI*, p. 3, start of system 6

introduce a D that, although implicit in the voice-leading of Ex. IV.1, was not actually sounded. Having thus brought to the fore a bare fifth, Berio deletes the first chord below C (which in Ex. IV.1 was itself a chord of fifths), and proceeds directly to the second, which also contains a D and a G. He then spells out the missing F♯ in the subsequent chord (the shift in harmonic texture while maintaining maximum harmonic identity is typical), and deletes the rest of the material from Ex. IV.1.

As this miniature example shows, the procedures that Berio employs for reworking a harmonic 'text' in *Sequenza VI* are closely related to those that we have already seen employed for melodic structures (cf. Exx. III.1–3). But the processes that he brings into play when allowing such a text to accrete new materials around it, as in *Chemins II*, are more complex. Here, in the main, the 'text' is itself not modified. But the accretions that grow from it, or are placed in counterpoint to it, are often such as to displace areas of harmonic and textural density, and thus to reshape the work's contours. This is particularly marked in *Chemins II*, for whereas in *Chemins I* the harp stands over against the orchestra as soloist, and in *Chemins IV* the oboe line of *Sequenza VII* forms a natural contrast with the surrounding string ensemble, here the solo viola line is often on the point of being engulfed by the dense network of instruments surrounding it. The nine instrumentalists involved have varying functions in relation to the soloist. For much of the time, the electronic organ acts as a sort of continuo, filling in the four-part harmony of the *Sequenza's* first four pages even where the viola itself only implies it. Marimbaphone and vibraphone at first add their weight to this central core, fleshing it out with an abundance of extra attacks and upbeat gestures, as does the harp. By contrast, viola and cello infiltrate the solo line from the start, creating denser harmonies within and around this harmonic core: and the harp and pitched percussion are drawn increasingly into this process. From this dense harmonic core, autonomous contrapuntal lines spin off—consigned in the main to the three wind instruments, flute, clarinet, and trombone.

To illustrate these processes, it may be as well to return to the same small section of harmonic material examined in Exx. IV.1 and 3. The first variant of that material (occuring in *Sequenza VI* at 2.6.) is set out in Ex. IV.4 as it appears in *Chemins II* (at H_{1-7}). In order to focus upon harmonic and dynamic essentials it is presented in short score, and the constant tremolandos, played by

Ex. IV.4 *Chemins II*, reduction of bars H1–7

all non-woodwind throughout, are omitted. Those notes played by the solo viola are given in white note-heads. (The original passage in the *Sequenza* was even more compressed: the viola leapt from the first chord to a hybrid chord in which notes from

49

the final chord below B were instead played beneath a B♭, and thence straight on to C.)

The initial chord is enriched in a characteristic way: strings, harp, and marimba add two notes that fill out its rather stark contours, and provide it with the third-/fourth-based colouration. The same process is at work on the second chord, momentarily heard in its original form, with its hint of G minor, before being engulfed in a dense superposition of the triads of G♭ and G. A similar filling process is at work in the third chord. As the solo viola stops playing, the rest of the ensemble fill in the missing B chords without further harmonic elaboration, while the woodwind declare independence, etching out an ascent to a held E♭—the final goal of each of these ascents, though one that in this particular instance is not to be reached (cf. Ex. IV.2). Beneath it the harmonic texture clears rapidly, with only the trombone complicating the fifth-based chord beneath C. The final four chords beneath C are infiltrated by a single, sustained harmonic object (in fact an E major triad from strings and trombone). With four notes out of seven static (leaving aside the semi-independent flute line) the ear is invited to relish the subtle changes in harmonic texture created by semitonal shifts in the three mobile parts. The dynamic curve of this static element also ensures that the third of the four chords is now a focal point—a role that it certainly did not play within the original sequence.

That same process of creating interaction between a dynamic entity and a static one can be seen on a slightly larger scale in Ex. IV.5, which shows how Ex. IV.3 fares within this more complex context. (Again, the tremolandos of solo viola, vibraphone, and marimbaphone are omitted, as are the ensemble viola and cello, who retune their accordatura quietly in the background.) Here, the persistent presence of the G/D fifth within the original harmonic sequence triggers a chord from harp, marimba, and vibraphone which adds a further fifth (D/A), and carries on upwards in diminished fifths (since A, as usual, activates E♭). Within this static frame of reference, the rising upper note of the original sequence moves from dissonance to gap-filling consonance (a function complemented by the woodwind's A♭). Meanwhile the trombone does a sort of ghost dance around the bass line of the viola part, half counterpoint, half heterophony.

Having responded to the harmonic challenge of the opening part of *Sequenza VI* with such vigorous complexity, Berio resorts

Ex. IV.5 *Chemins II*, reduction of bars K4–8

to simpler means as the texture of the solo viola line moves towards melody. It will be recalled that at 4.1 in Ex. IV.2 the first fixed field of *Sequenza VI* was reduced from ten notes to eight, and then momentarily to six before launching into the melodic version of the ascent. Berio now siezes upon those six notes to form a static, though texturally rich, backdrop against which the solo viola can at last achieve a measure of autonomy. From time to time the backdrop is changed, and within it pitch conjunctions with the solo part are emphasized. But essentially we are now listening to discrete layers.

This process of dissociation reaches its logical conclusion at a point just prior to the pause which in *Sequenza VI*, separated off the static pitch fields of the final section. Here the ensemble declares independence from the solo part, and interrupts briefly though vehemently with a chromatically saturated block of sound. Similar interruptions, reshaping the relatively docile character and contours of the final section of *Sequenza VI*, occur just before the establishing of the last pitch field and at the very end. In effect, the anarchic interpenetration between viola and ensemble of the opening has resolved itself into a more traditional polarization.

As an essay in the control of harmonic and textural density, *Chemins II* was one of Berio's most formidable achievements to date. He seemed well aware of its significance, and in each of the next two years he returned to it to provide a further reworking or commentary. The first of these, *Chemins III* (1968), sought in principle to extend the process initiated by *Chemins II*, to whose resources it added a full orchestra. Berio was fond of likening *Sequenza VI*, embedded in *Chemins II*, embedded in *Chemins III* to the layers of an onion. In practice, had the harmonic proliferation accomplished in *Chemins II* been allowed to multiply itself further, the resultant density would have been aurally impenetrable. So the first version of *Chemins III* was compelled to deploy the orchestra with a certain caution. Indeed, when in 1973 Berio decided to reshape the work for viola and orchestra, he resolved the problem with what is, in effect, an able orchestration of *Chemins II*. String and percussion textures are somewhat thickened out, and the three wind parts are 'scattered' among several instruments. Here and there new fragments of wind counterpoint are added—well away from the already dense harmonic core. But only at one point does *Chemins III* substantially modify the model established by *Chemins II*. It will be recalled that at T_1 of *Chemins II*, the point at which the structural principles governing the work are about to change, the ensemble made the first of three brief interruptions. This now becomes a major confrontation between viola and orchestra, with the soloist developing materials from its next entry and from the closing bars. Thus what was a point of relative inertia in *Sequenza VI* has developed a density rivalling the opening: the large-scale contours of the work have in effect been re-thought.

For much of the opening part of *Chemins II*, the solo viola line of *Sequenza VI* was well-nigh engulfed by the proliferating commentary around it. While working on *Opera* between 1969 and 1970, Berio pushed this process one step further, and in *Chemins IIb* dissolved the solo viola line entirely into a large, wind-dominated ensemble. This striking demonstration of Berio's skill in transcription used almost precisely the same idiosyncratic ensemble that he was concurrently exploring in *Opera*. With much increased wind and brass at his disposal, Berio was able to transform the familiar string and percussion tremolandos into a ferocious barrage of rapid tonguing, rather after the manner of *Epifanie D*. To this in 1972 he finally added an optional solo line for bass clarinet to form *Chemins IIc*; but the new line is relatively ancillary to the musical argument, and the work has not often been heard in this form.

The technique of commentary by harmonic enrichment that forms the basis of the various *Chemins* found an almost immediate extension in Berio's next major work, *Sinfonia* (1968–9) for an orchestra incorporating eight amplified voices. Some of the vocal and verbal aspects of this work will be discussed in the next chapter. But the harmonic processes at work in the second, third, and fifth movements have their place here. *Sinfonia* is a classic example of Berio's affection for seeking out relationships between apparently disparate projects. Its first movement plays complex verbal games with fragments from Claude Lévi-Strauss's *Le cru et le cuit*; its second movement reworks *O King*, discussed in Chapters III and V; its third movement elaborates a complex commentary upon the scherzo of Mahler's Second Symphony; and its fourth movement provides a quiet postlude. It was thus that it was first performed in 1968. Berio then decided to add a fifth movement that synthesized these disparate elements, quite literally making them 'sound together', as the title, translated from the Greek, would imply. On a semantic level these movements were united by images of water and death. But to give a sense of overall shape on a musical level, Berio had to rely on a careful control of harmonic density. The first movement uses a small number of third-based chords as a background to its verbal games, before resolving into a monody based upon reworkings of a pitch-class sequence. In incorporating *O King* into *Sinfonia*, Berio had to bridge the gap between the harmonic simplicity of the first movement, and the complexity of the third. As was noted in the last chapter, the projections from the rotating pitch sequence of *O King* provided a constantly shifting, but limited harmonic vocabulary. So while maintaining *O King* intact as a nucleus, much as *Sequenza VI* had been in *Chemins II*, Berio quietly enriched that vocabulary by assigning pitches excluded from the cycle to the lower voices and instruments, and thus created an interaction with the pitch processes of the central core not unlike that of Ex. IV.4. But where *Chemins II* shows the almost explosive potential of these commentary techniques when intensively applied, the second movement of *Sinfonia* uses them with the utmost restaint.

The scene is thus set for the third movement—a famous and remarkable experiment whose very popularity has tended to distort perceptions of Berio's relationship to the music of the past. It was a natural consequence of the widening of harmonic vocabulary discussed in the previous chapter that Berio should begin to scrutinize the relationships between tonal praxis and his own post-tonal resources. In 1965 he had written a small piano piece, *Wasserklavier*, exploring skeletal harmonic gestures from the tradition of Brahms and Schubert; and in the same year had introduced into *Laborintus II* a 'Canzonetta', whose madrigalian texture offered a brief *hommage* to Monteverdi. As his commentary techniques consolidated, he therefore considered applying them to a classical 'text'. Possible candidates were the final three movements of Beethoven's Op. 131, and the second movement of Mahler's Second Symphony. But he settled instead on the scherzo from that Symphony. Had he used only his own harmonic resources to generate projections from this predominantly diatonic basis, the discrepancy between text and commentary would have been too great. So to bridge that gap, he also used materials taken from other composers' works. Although pre-Mahlerian composers were occasionally evoked, much of the movement ranged from the relatively sumptuous harmony of Strauss, Ravel, and Debussy, through Schoenberg, Berg, and Stravinsky to his own massive, chromatically saturated orchestral clusters, discussed in Chapter II.

Clearly, in this instance he could not follow the example of *Chemins II*, and leave Mahler's scherzo intact at the core of the movement: to have done so would have made for impossibly dense textures (and an impossibly large orchestra). So he blocked out some of the original material—at first so as to make room, but increasingly as an autonomous process so that by the end we are left with a Mahlerian skeleton. Only very late in the day, though, does he start to dismember Mahler's bar structure: until then fragments re-emerge where they would have done had the scherzo been audible all along.

Berio thus creates an exceptionally rich ebb and flow of harmonic density: a more wide-ranging equivalent to that at work in *Chemins II*. But because he is bringing together materials from disparate sources, he has to focus upon ways in which one *objet trouvé* may trigger another. This may be a straightforward matter of similarity. A given melodic gesture or harmonic process is 'multiplied out' into other, similar, superimposed materials from different sources. This naturally makes for a situation of relative harmonic density, since such materials are then allowed to go their separate ways. On the other hand, Berio often counterpoints materials with common pitch elements, so that one maps partially on to the other. It is this latter technique that is to become central in the fifth movement.

The examples of musical commentary so far discussed have had a single text as their focus. But in the last movement of *Sinfonia* Berio interleaves materials from all the previous movements. At first he does so by exploring harmonic contiguities; then, by taking the central line of *O King* as a focus for ever denser harmonic accretions. But such dense harmonies can only be heard globally, and in the final section of the movement Berio devises a means of leading the ear into a more detailed exploration by writing a single undulating pitch line, running up and down through the whole gamut of the orchestra, and 'spelling out' its harmonic content as it goes.[3]

Thus at the start of the seventies Berio had to hand two possible approaches to complex harmony. On the one hand he could encourage the listener to percieve globally and intuitively by presenting each aggregate as a simultaneity—often just a staccato attack. On the other, he could invite the listener to delve into a harmonic process by spelling it out in a continuous *arpeggiando* whose harmonic implications were then selectively explored in a manner similar to *O King*. Each approach was to generate a more extended orchestral 'study'. First came *Bewegung* in 1971. This took up where the final monody of *Sinfonia* had left off. But where in *Sinfonia* the central line had juggled between several interrelated fixed pitch sequences, in *Bewegung* it spelt out a slowly evolving fixed pitch field. (The title means 'movement', and presumably applies as much to the harmonic level as it does to the quiet, crotchet and quaver flow of the central line.) Although the whole orchestra is employed in picking out selective resonances, it encourages aural concentration by playing *sempre ppp*. The second study, since withdrawn as an autonomous work, was *Still* (1973), a concentrated examination of staccato orchestral aggregates, likewise *sempre ppp*. Here Berio was able to explore at length the subtle differences in harmonic texture created by altering one or two notes within a vast chord, or gaps within otherwise saturated clusters. Equally, he was able to repeat the same aggregate a number of times while swapping notes between instruments so as to create just perceptible differences in the global timbre of the aggregate. This fascination with working at the limits of perception (and well beyond most listeners' capacities for aural analysis) was a pervasive feature of Berio's work during this period: it will be equally evident when examining his relationship to the voice in the next chapter.

Drawing upon his experience in the final movement of *Sinfonia*, Berio now took these two processes and combined them. Although he named the resultant work *Eindrücke* (literally 'imprints' or 'traces'), it is by no means a mosaic of fragments from its two antecedents. Instead, the quiet, irregular attacks of *Still* are used as a grid, through which the central pitch line of *Bewegung* weaves, its brisk, square-cut rhythms transformed into a sinuous, irregular progress coloured by constant changes of instrumental timbre. Berio continues this process until he has worked his way right through *Still*—by which time approximately half of *Bewegung*'s central line has been thus reworked. Around it, as before, harmonic echoes proliferate, but these now dissolve into trills, or establish momentarily independent lines. Even *Still*'s staccato attacks develop into stuttering repetitions.

The start of this process is illustrated in Ex. IV.6, a reduction of the opening bars of *Eindrücke* with the equivalent portion of the central line from *Bewegung* placed above it. The equivalent portion of *Still* follows the pattern of attacks notated on the bottom two staves, but uses only repetitions of the fifth chord minus its bottom two notes, with a G added for the final two chords (though the chord undergoes continual alterations in its

Ex. IV.6a *Bewegung*, central melody only (cf. piano), bars 1–4, and
b *Eindrücke*, reduction of bars 1–6

internal instrumentation, as described above). Clearly, in *Eindrücke* this chord is not only extended downwards, but is constantly modified by its encounters with the pitch line of the top stave, which tends to hollow out a space around it. On the second stave are encapsulated the pitch projections and commentaries thrown off by the main line. These include not only selective anticipations and resonances but also, in bar 2, the filling of a gap in the pitch line (immediately echoed by the subsequent attack) and, in bar 4, a quasi-organum using adjacent pitches within the fixed field. In bars 3, 4, and 6 the staccato attacks also generate resonances.

Bewegung and *Eindrücke* mark the establishment of an important evolution in Berio's work: a deliberate stepping aside from the vivid idiom of the *Sequenzas* and the vocal works of the sixties to focus upon problems of musical language. The rich, but semi-anarchic harmonic processes at work in *Sequenza IV*, *Sequenza VI*, or *Chemins II* now gave way to a more disciplined assertion of technical control. *Linea* (1973), *Calmo*, and *Points on the Curve to Find...* (both 1974), all consolidated the same conception. *Calmo* stands somewhat apart from the others, in that the central vocal line unfolds through the familiar process of reinterpreting its initial melodic statements. But the most incisive (and subsequently the most frequently performed) of these studies in harmony and texture is *Points on the Curve to Find*.... Here the undulating *perpetuum mobile* of the central piano line activates around it a sort of harmonic kaleidoscope that constantly inflects the same circumscribed harmonic resources in new ways. The basic pitch process at work in the piano line is of disarming simplicity. The twelve notes of the scale are set out in the fixed order shown in Ex. IV.7. The piano line starts with a cycle that uses the first ten of these. The continuous demisemiquavers hover, oscillating between two notes, then carry on round the cycle to hover again on another two (thus creating a basic melodic progression similar to that of Ex. IV.6). When all ten diads have thus provided a moment of melodic stasis, the piano begins a game of registral transpositions (at 1.2), and again exhausts all diads in a different order. This accomplished, at 3 the whole cycle shifts, discarding

Ex. IV.7 Pitch cycle for *Point on the Curve to Find* . . .

the D and adding the B♭. Within this new cycle, the piano pauses over diads in the same order as before (and since these moments of stasis are of greatly varying length, new pitch relations are brought to the fore). At 4.12, the cycle shifts again, discarding the C♯ and adding the G. At 6.7 the F is in turn discarded, and the D re-enters the cycle. And so on. The pattern of expansion and contraction, as each cycle starts in 'close' formation and then expands into other registers, is echoed at least in part by the commentaries that spin off from this central line. In effect, what is created is a sort of developing variation form, allowing Berio to display an almost Brahmsian delight in creating variety out of an underlying unity.

This withdrawal into the musical workshop allowed Berio to develop a sureness of touch in his handling of a broad harmonic palette that bore fruit in the rich complexity of *Ritorno degli snovidenia* (1977), to be discussed in Chapter VI, and in the major theatrical works of the late seventies and early eighties, to be discussed in Chapter VII. Clearly, such 'learned' works could be expected to engage only a relatively sophisticated audience. But alongside them Berio was writing large-scale works destined for the same broad range of listeners that had been attracted to *Circles* or *Sinfonia*, notably the *Concerto* for two pianos and orchestra of 1972–3, and *Coro* of 1975–6. Discussion of the latter must wait until Chapter VI, but the *Concerto* offers a compendium of many of the techniques discussed in this and the previous chapter. Its overtly sectional structure, clear reminiscences of past works (*Sequenza IV* in the profusion of dense staccato chords from the pianos, *Sequenza VI* in the episode for solo violin, *Laborintus II* and *Sinfonia* in the solo flute episode) and of techniques past and present (fixed fields in the violin and clarinet episodes, proliferation from a central line in the orchestral episode) all make of the *Concerto* a clear example of Berio's 'encyclopaedic' work: a summing up before moving on.

V
FROM WORDS TO MUSIC

The distinctive vocal style that Berio created in the sixties has received more critical attention, and attracted more imitators than any other part of his work. Its durable impact owes a good deal to an all-embracing delight in the voice and its resources. But here as elsewhere in Berio's work, that apparently spontaneous exuberance exists in tension with a wider and more systematic perspective. Berio delves into texts to find in them elements, whether phonetic or semantic, that may be used as structural components in their own right. However remarkable his flair for the telling individual gesture, it is this sense of structural perspective that gives his vocal works their richness and resilience.

However, the seminal works of the early sixties were written not for 'the voice', but for a voice: that of Cathy Berberian. Berberian's vocal career had gone somewhat into abeyance in the mid-fifties: the first performance of *Chamber Music* in 1953 was the last that she gave before the birth of her daughter, Christina. Apart from some minor recordings for radio, she devoted the next few years to looking after her child. But she was determined to return to singing, and in 1958 relaunched her career in Naples during the second series of *Incontri Musicali* concerts, where she performed Stravinsky and Ravel. Soon she was at work on a more challenging repertoire, for in that year John Cage came to Milan to make *Fontana Mix* at the *Studio di fonologia*. Since he was staying in a modest *pensione*, he frequently ate with the Berios, and amused by Berberian's domestic vocal clowning, decided to write something for her. She gave him texts which he then broke up, and formed into a collage that compelled her to jump from one vocal style to another. The result, *Aria*, was performed in Rome with *Fontana Mix* later that year, and in the summer of 1959 Berberian took *Aria* to Darmstadt. In that year she also gave the première of Bussotti's *Voix de femme* from *Pièces de chair*.

But while Berberian was developing her distinctive style of vocal theatre Berio was consolidating an approach to the voice within which individual gestures could contribute something more than anecdotal detail. His work at the RAI had brought him into contact with a number of talented young writers: among them, Umberto Eco, with whom he developed a close friendship. By 1957, they were pursuing shared enthusiasms: Eco introduced Berio to the complexities of Joyce's *Ulysses*,[1] and Berio set Eco on the track of de Saussure's linguistics. One product of this cross-fertilization was a radio programme that they planned together entitled *Onomatopea nel linguaggio poetico* (onomatopoeia in poetic language). This at first was intended to cover a range of writers including Poe, Dylan Thomas and Auden. Although the final version of the programme included extracts from all of these read by Berberian, the project was quickly fined down to an intensive study of one specific passage from *Ulysses*: the 'overture' from the 'Sirens' chapter. Berio by now could see his way towards deriving a purely musical structure from this text. He recorded Berberian's marvellously apt reading of it; he also recorded French and Italian translations of the same section using mixed voices. By creating counterpoints out of these, first within each language, then electronically transforming this mixture, he hoped to lead the listener step by step over the border between sense and sound: but the result proved too challenging, and was never broadcast. He therefore set about making an autonomous, and more focused tape piece, *Thema* (*Omaggio a Joyce*), which was based entirely on Berberian's reading of Joyce's original text.

Berio's involvement with this particular passage from *Ulysses* was to have consequences far beyond *Thema* itself. One of the many factors governing the macrostructure of *Ulysses* is the association of each chapter with one of the arts: that of the 'Sirens' chapter is music. This not only gave Joyce the opportunity to raise the alliterative and onomatopoeic qualities of his prose to their highest pitch, and to weave a prodigious number of song quotations into the narrative, it also encouraged him in the somewhat fanciful conceit of viewing the various entrances and exits that enliven the Ormond Bar at lunchtime as a *fuga per canonem*. His 'overture' to the chapter takes up a technique first hinted at in the 'Wandering Rocks' chapter, where an isolated and apparently alien phrase will appear in the midst of the narrative, only to reveal its significance when the reader passes on to another section, and there finds it in its own context (a device used by Joyce to suggest the simultaneity of two events in different parts of Dublin). The 'overture' to the 'Sirens' chapter frees this process from any narrative function. It consists entirely of dislocated phrases from the ensuing narration. These tell no story, so there is nothing to distract the reader from texture and rhythm—save that the mind, confronted with isolated images, begins to build hypothetical bridges between them, generating new meanings quite unrelated to those that each fragment is to adopt in the ensuing narrative.

Joyce's example was to be put to abundant use in Berio's future work. But in *Thema* (*Omaggio a Joyce*) (*thema*, or 'theme' because he viewed the 'overture' as setting out the themes of the ensuing *fuga per canonem*), the focus was instead upon extending the process initiated by Joyce to its logical conclusion. Joyce had extracted from his musicalized narrative a mosaic that developed its own semantic and musical potentials. Berio now extracted from that mosaic purely musical elements, and used them to explore the borderline where sound as the bearer of linguistic sense dissolves into sound as the bearer of musical meaning: a territory that over the next decade he was to make very much his own. In part he did this by taking Joyce's polyphonic imagery literally, and superposing texts upon themselves with slightly different rhythmic spacings: in effect, translating text into texture. But the operation that provided the key to much of his future vocal work was an analysis of Berberian's recording that grouped words from the text in terms of their phonetic content.

Phonetic material can be analysed in two ways: either in terms of its acoustic structure, or in terms of the positions that the mouth and throat must take up in order to form it. (The two do not necessarily map on to each other in any straightforward way.) In view of his intensive work in the *Studio di fonologia* at this time, it might have seemed natural to adopt the former approach. Indeed, had he chosen to combine vocal and electronic materials, as had Stockhausen in *Gesang der Jünglinge* two years before, such an approach would have been necessary. But unlike Stockhausen, Berio had opted to work entirely with his vocal recordings, and so he chose to sort out his materials in strictly articulatory terms. He grouped isolated words from Joyce's text according to their vowel content, and arranged these groups as a 'series' determined by the position in the mouth used to articulate each vowel. But if the constraints of 'natural' articulation provided him with a way of ordering his material, he then proceded to work in tension with it, juxtaposing and superposing phonetic elements so as to produce consonant groupings that the human voice would normally find hard to articulate in rapid succession (such as voiced and unvoiced plosives).[2]

Out of this 'impossible' vocalism, comprehensible speech (usually a single word) momentarily emerges, only to be engulfed: relative comprehensibility has become a compositional parameter to be handled in much the same way as textural density or, within a pitched context, harmonic density. In one form or another, and with the sole exception of the more lyrical settings in *Epifanie*, this has remained a constant of Berio's vocal style. It may be achieved by the fragmentation of originally linear texts, as Joyce did in assembling his 'overture', by superposition of texts, as Berio did in the initial stages of work on *Thema*, by dissolution of texts into their component phonetic materials, or more usually by a combination of these.

By focusing upon the phonetic borderline that divides sense from sound, and upon relative comprehensibility as a structural component, *Thema* set the agenda for Berio's handling of language within music over a long period to come. It also focused the attention of his closest associates upon similar concerns: Pousseur's electronic ballet *Electre* (1960) derived its materials exclusively from the speaking voice, and Maderna's *Dimensioni II* of the same year sought to explore the potential of purely phonetic materials derived from a variety of languages, and combined as a phonetic 'text' by Hans G. Helms. In one respect, *Dimensioni II* (whose title harks back to *Musica su due dimensioni*, discussed in Chapter II) provides a conceptual stepping-stone between *Thema*, and Berio's next electronic/vocal project, *Visage* (1960–61). Helms's text had to be turned into recorded sound, and Maderna therefore asked Cathy Berberian to read it, infusing it with whatever intonations her imagination might suggest. In *Visage* Berio went one step further. He dispensed with texts altogether, and allowed Berberian's fertile imagination its head. In the recording studio, she improvised a series of monologues, each based on a repertoire of vocal gesture and phonetic material suggested by a given linguistic model, but in fact using no words from that language. Yet like any foreign conversation overheard in a train or a café, they were far from meaningless, and graphically conveyed 'content' by gesture and intonation. (One exhausting session was devoted entirely to different types of laughter, an obsession to which Berio was to return in *Sequenza III*). Only one real word was included: 'parole', the Italian for 'words', which is precisely what everything around it was not. Out of these materials Berio built a montage so rich in suggestions of psychological drama that the RAI, for whom the work was originally intended, banned the work from the air-waves as 'obscene'. To this central core he then added electronic sounds that extended reflections of Berberian's voice into a further 'dimension'—though one that in due course turns viciously upon the hapless protagonist.

The musical potentials that Berio had detected within articulatory phonetics depended in large part upon characteristics that had only recently developed within the discipline. Due in large measure to the pioneering work of Daniel Jones and the International Phonetic Association, post-war phoneticians had at their disposal a fairly compact and elegant system of analysis. The phonetic alphabet that they produced proposed a set of 'cardinal vowels' which they arranged as a matrix governed by two fundamental oppositions: resonance at the front of the mouth versus resonance at the back, and closed mouth versus open. In a second matrix they set out 'secondary cardinal vowels' where the same tongue positions are modified by less commonly associated lip positions. Consonants, on the other hand, could not be reduced to a two-dimensional matrix because they depend upon at least three basic features: front articulation versus back, stopping of air-flow (plosives) versus relatively unrestricted air-flow (nasals and laterals), and voiced versus unvoiced. They were therefore set out according to the front–back opposition.[3]

The merits of this phonetic alphabet from the musician's point of view were twofold: first, it provided a reasonably accurate means of notating speech sounds, and second, it offered a series of discrete elements organized within a structured system, and thus potentially open to ordering in purely formal terms. Berio had used the alphabet's notational potential to plan and 'score' *Thema*. But although the phonetic alphabet made a brief appearence in *Circles* (1960) at the point of maximum semantic disintegration, it was not until he began work on *Sequenza III* in 1965 that he took up once more the structural implications of the IPA's alphabet. His starting-point was a 'modular' text supplied for him by Markus Kutter ('modular' only in appearance, since its nine apparently disjointed phrases can be read sequentially as a brief but conventional poem that expands upon Berio's invitation to Kutter: 'give me a few words for a woman to sing', etc.). Kutter's 'few words' are never heard in anything like their original order: Berio treats them simply as a quarry for phonetic materials, out of which from time to time a coherent phrase is allowed to emerge, rather after the manner of *Thema*.

The play of phonetic materials has as its framework the articulatory polarities defined in the IPA's alphabet. Consonants are frequently grouped in oppositional pairs governed by one or more of the three features outlined above. Vowels, too, may be treated in this way, but they offer more interesting possibilities when considered in relation to the front–back/open–closed matrix. Especially in the earlier part of the work, Berio selects chains of vowels that set up a circular motion around this matrix (as for example in the second and third 'distant and dreamy' sections on the first page of the score which, after initial quirks, proceed anticlockwise). In turn circularity allows games with direction, for which the minimum requirements are three different points around the matrix. Much of the first system of page 2 translates into such games, as can be seen from Ex. V.1. Here an initial front closed [i]—front open [a]—back closed [u] sequence (completed by the central closed /si/ of 'sing') is immediately reversed. Then it is repeated, with 'a few' instead of [a] [u] (here the intermediate 'a' takes the place of [a]). The text intervenes briefly with /wor/ of 'words', then there is a final, spun-out reversal, with [u] replaced by its neighbouring back near-closed [o].

This display of oral acrobatics continues throughout the piece, and is complemented by a rapid alternation between types of voice production, and between ways of delivering the text (forty-four different directions to the singer are used, most of them

Ex. V.1 *Sequenza III*, p. 2, most of system 1

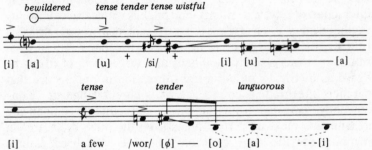

invoking a psychological state). Sometimes these three layers collude, sometimes they collide. They are constantly punctuated by laughter. (In the initial version, the list of different types of laughter required was dauntingly long.) The constant flux in vocal behaviour that results has tempted critics into all sorts of psychiatric interpretations. But Berio deploys Berberian's extraordinary agility not in order to precipitate psychological drama, but to review this kaleidoscope of vocal behaviours with a fascinated detachment, each temptation to empathy being instantly countered by the next.

A more disciplined interaction between phonetic structures and other parameters is to be found in Berio's next vocal piece *O King*, composed in 1967. In that year, Martin Luther King was murdered, and Berio felt impelled to respond. The chamber work that resulted, *O King*, took as its text a simple apostrophe: 'O Martin Luther King', that is gradually assembled from its phonetic components as the piece proceeds. Berio starts with all the vowels from this text, and assembles them in anticlockwise order; he then separates them into two anticlockwise triangles of the sort discussed above in relation to *Sequenza III*, follows this with a clockwise and an anticlockwise triangle, and finally states the two clockwise triangles that form the correct vowel sequence of the text. (As an additional *tour de force*, this whole process yields equal structural sense when analysed as permutation of the final vowel order.) With the vowels in place, Berio starts to add consonants, proceding from the vowel-like voiced consonants to the more disruptive, unvoiced ones. As the text nears completion, processes in other parameters provoke a climax, after which the work closes with a single full statement of the text.

This linear phonetic process interacts with a number of others to create the macro-structure of *O King*. As was noted in Chapter III, the central pitch line of this work is generated by the interaction of a cycle of twenty-one pitches with a cycle of twenty rhythmic units. Each of these is in turn subject to a larger process. Initially, the rhythmic cycle has an additive basis, but at each return it is increasingly modified until large parts of it can be heard as metrically based: a transformation in perspective that parallels the gradual emergence of coherent language. Concurrently, *sforzandi* from the piano and other accompanying instruments pick out certain notes from the pitch cycle, in fact mapping out the same cycle on a macrocosmic level. Unlike phonetics and rhythm, this is potentially a closed, self-perpetuating process, but just as it threatens to start repeating itself, and the rhythmic cycle to become unyieldingly metric, Berio breaks out of both cycles, and precipitates a climax. Finally, the shifting harmonic cloud created around the central line by the instrumental ensemble becomes progressively denser as the piece procedes, an accretive process that mirrors the build-up of phonetic materials, just as rhythm had mirrored the change from phonemes to language.[4]

O King marks a high point in Berio's use of phonetic relationships as a structural parameter. Thereafter, the extraction of phonetic elements from a text takes its place as one of a number of devices used to establish greater or lesser degrees of semantic continuity. Thus in *Evo* (1972) the Sicilian lullaby used as a text is first presented in linear form and then, as it begins to repeat, troped by phonetic interludes. Particularly when placed within the dramatic context of *Opera* (see Chapter VII), this process serves to underline the tension between the text and the darker, more complex lament created from it. Indeed, in his major theatrical works from the mid-seventies on, Berio acknowledges the psychological interpretation that we would normally put upon semi-coherent speech, and uses dissolution into phonetic materials as a sign of extreme mental tension, as in the role of Passante III (Third Passer-by) from the second act of *La vera storia* (1977–81) or the Protagonista who appears at the end of *Un re in ascolto* (1979–84). But in general semantic discontinuity, though always a challenge to the listener, carries with it no specific psychological connotations.

There are three levels on which Berio challenges semantic continuity in his response to texts. The first is the interface between words as bearers of meaning and words as sound materials, already discussed in part above. The second is the simultaneous use of different texts. And the third is the deliberate use of texts whose meaning is fragmentary or incomplete. Each can be used as a contribution to the overall structural design, but entails different considerations.

The *locus classicus* for the first of these is *Circles*, written for Cathy Berberian in 1960. Here the text is dissolved into its phonetic components only very briefly, but exploration of the sonorous qualities of the text is central to the work's structure. *Circles* is written for mezzo-soprano, harp, and two percussionists.

Each percussionist is surrounded by a circle of instruments divided between the three families of wood, skin, and metal (set out in that order, moving from outside to centre, in the score), and covering the full range between exact pitch (vibraphone, marimbaphone, etc.) through relative pitch (sets of temple-blocks, tom-toms, etc.) to individual unpitched sounds (sand-block, tam-tam, glass chimes, etc.). The voice responds with a similar range, moving from exactly pitched song through approximate pitch to speech, while the harp allies itself now with the voice, now with the pitched percussion.

The texts that these resources are used to explore are three poems by e. e. cummings, each more discontinuous than the last. There are five settings in all, since poems two and one return to complete one of many circles. The first poem, 'stinging', offers a sequence of images focused upon sun, spires, bells (only the last line expands beyond them). This semantic continuity is mirrored by the melismatic flow of its setting: a duo for voice and harp. But from the start there are hints of what is to come. The harp responds to the phonetic substance of the poem with what Berio describes as a series of 'pitched plosives': the unison attacks that echo the /st/ and /g/ of 'stinging' and 'gold'. This mimetic interaction between voice and instruments comes closer to the foreground in the second setting. Here the text, 'riverly is a flower', displays more fragmented imagery and contorted grammar. It is matched by a more syllabic vocal setting that incorporates other vocal timbres into what is still basically a *cantabile* line, set against a background of trills and flurries from harp and pitched wood. But these trills are in fact an echo of the many fricatives in the text, notably the initial /r/s of 'riverly' and 'rosily'. Nor do instruments merely echo the voice. Bongos on page 10 of the score introduce a gesture that is echoed by the voice on the word 'befall', and then carry on developing it: there is simply a momentary intersection.

Such details as these could be multiplied *ad infinitum* in the third section. cummings's text, 'n(o)w', deploys highly eccentric punctuation and stray capital letters to suggest an imminent dissolution into its phonetic parts. Such jitters are appropriate: the poem evokes a thunderstorm and its sunny aftermath. Berio responds in kind, unleashing the full range of Berberian's resources, echoed and answered by the percussionists, so that sense does indeed stand on the brink of dissolving into sound. (It is, though, a measure of Berio's confident sense of historical continuity that he should fear no danger in contributing a further chapter to the history of the musical thunderstorm: it is hard to think who else among the Darmstadt generation might have undertaken this in 1960, let alone carry it off with such bravura.)

That dissolution does not actually come, however, until the end of the third setting where the singer extracts phonetic materials from the poem that she has just sung, and presents them in a rough retrograde, echoed by the percussionists. This heralds the start of a large-scale retrograde process, as 'riverly is a flower' is reset in section IV and 'stinging' in section V. These settings in turn spark off a multitude of circular processes. 'riverly is a flower' is now set to the voice and harp duo of I. Indeed, the vocal line of the first part of IV reworks the initial pitch sequence from I as a cycle. By the second part it has moved on to rework pitch sequences from the original setting of the text in II (cf. pages 10 and 11). This brief résumé is completed in V by spoken patterns derived from III (cf. pages 22–3 and 18 of the score), and retrogrades of the repeated percussion attacks from the same movement (cf. pages 15, 18, 19, and 26). Meanwhile, the percussionists underpin the retrograde in the text: having moved from pitched wood in II to mixed attacks in III, they await the mention of 'rain' in IV to re-enter with similar mixed attacks before reverting to pitched percussion in V, this time predominantly metal. Voice-production adds its own retrograde in V, maintaining a mixture of syllabic song and speech similar to II until, at 'ringing with rose' it breaks into a melisma that reworks its original setting in I. Thereafter the voice maintains melismatic song to the end. Even visually, Berio plays with circular forms, setting the percussionists into frantic gyrations around their instruments in III, requiring the singer to move in a half circle from her initial position in front of the instrumentalists until she is absorbed into the ensemble, and in the last few bars asking the second percussionist to trace circles in the air with a clap-cymbal. This polyphony of circular processes is summarized in Ex. V.2[5]

There is, however, one brief disruption of the progress back to semantic coherence in the second half of *Circles*. The mention of 'rain' in IV triggers echoes of the previous storm: not only the re-entry of percussion, but also a temporary reversion to discontinuity, as cummings's poem is broken into isolated phrases sung/spoken in a spasmodic counterpoint by the vocalist and the

Ex. V.2 Cyclic processes in *Circles*

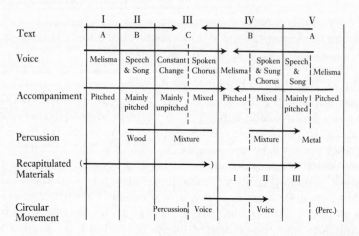

	I	II	III		IV		V	
Text	A	B	C		B		A	
Voice	Melisma	Speech & Song	Constant Change	Spoken Chorus	Melisma	Spoken & Sung Chorus	Speech & Song	Melisma
Accompaniment	Pitched	Mainly pitched	Mainly unpitched	Mixed	Pitched	Mixed	Mainly pitched	Pitched
Percussion		Wood	Mixture			Mixture	Metal	
Recapitulated Materials	(————————————)				I	II	III	
Circular Movement			Percussion	Voice		Voice	(Perc.)	

two percussionists. No doubt the roots of this lie in the super-positions with which Berio experimented in *Thema*, but it was shortly to be developed into an autonomous device.

Circles and *Epifanie* were the last works in which Berio set complete and autonomous texts. Since then he has either fragmented pre-established texts (so as to make them 'open' to further creative work), or he has worked with a living writer, negotiating with him the shape that the words will take. The first, and in many ways the most seminal of these collaborations was with the poet and scholar, Edoardo Sanguineti. Sanguineti occupied a position in Italian literature similar to that of Maderna or Berio in music, in that he spent the early fifties assimilating and bringing new life to a radical (and mainly Anglo-Saxon) tradition that had found little chance to take root in Italy during previous decades. He took his inspiration from the experiments of Ezra Pound and early Eliot, employing a continuous flux of tense and person, of literary and colloquial styles, and of different languages to create a counterpoint of images made all the more vivid by the layout of the text, and a highly idiosyncratic style of punctuation. His first poem sequence, *Laborintus*, appeared in 1956, but he became more widely known when he joined with four other poets to found the 'Novissimi' group. The publication in 1961 of their manifesto in the form of an annotated selection of poems and essays unleashed considerable critical turmoil.

In the following year, Berio began to plan a theatre piece. He had already read and admired Sanguineti's work, and therefore sought him out to propose a collaboration. Together they produced *Passaggio*, a crucial work in the development of Berio's theatre, and therefore one best discussed in detail alongside his other theatrical works in Chapter VII. One of the more striking innovations of *Passaggio* should, however, be mentioned here. On stage Berio placed only a single female singer, but in the orchestra pit there was an eight-part choir alongside the instrumental ensemble, and scattered around the auditorium, five groups of speakers using a variety of languages. The singer enacted the bare outline of a dramatic progression—a woman captured, interrogated, and finally freed—while the choruses voiced a wide, and often contradictory gamut of responses in several different languages. With these resources in hand, Berio was able to contract the implicit semantic counterpoints of Sanguineti's earlier writing into genuine synchronicity. Different (though dramatically complementary) texts were often sung or shouted simultaneously: it was up to the listener to find his own path through the jungle.

The dramatic potential of this multi-voiced medium encouraged further experiment. While working on *Passaggio*, Berio and Sanguineti also put together for the Venice Biennale of 1963 a theatre piece, *Esposizione*, that replaced narrative with a montage of gestural and verbal fragments from Sanguineti's own work, and the *Etymologies* of Isidore of Seville (but again seized upon the possibilities of dramatizing aural space by positioning singers at different points around the theatre). This frankly exploratory work was quickly withdrawn, and its more striking materials reworked in *Laborintus II*. A year later, responding to a commission from the Library of Congress in Washington, Berio transfered confrontation to the concert hall with *Traces*, a work for voices, actors, choruses, and orchestra on a text by Susan Oyama that tackled the problematic subject of race relations. After a number of performances this too was withdrawn, though some of its materials re-emerged in *Opera* (1970).

But these works served to clarify Berio's vision of what could be achieved in a multi-voiced medium. So that when the ORTF commissioned a work from Berio and Sanguineti to celebrate the 700th anniversary of Dante's birth in 1965, he was able to exercise a striking economy and directness of gesture. Like *Passaggio*, this new work, named *Laborintus II* after Sanguineti's first collection of poems, employed three contrasting vocal layers —a solo speaker, three female singers, and eight speakers, all of them amplified so as to allow the full range of vocal nuance to be used alongside an instrumental ensemble. In putting together the text from Dante's writings—the *Vita Nuova*, the first nine Cantos of the *Inferno*, and, towards the end, a passage on music from the *Convivio*—Sanguineti employed a technique strongly reminiscent of that used by Joyce at the start of the Sirens chapter from *Ulysses*. He extracted a series of isolated images which, although striking in themselves, also represented in skeletal outline the narrations from which they came.[6] These he interlarded with other materials: rambling lists of information about Hebrew ancient history taken from the Latin of Isidore of Seville, to which he provided a modern counterpart in lists of incongruously juxtaposed facts and figures from contemporary life, brief quotations from Eliot and Pound (from the latter a well-known passage from *Canto XLV: With Usura* that is married to Dante's denunciation of usury from the *Inferno*), and more extensive materials from his own *Laborintus*, and *Purgatorio de l'Inferno*.

Fragments from this latter poem sequence end the work. In their original context, they provide an answer to the question of how Sanguineti, as a committed radical, justifies the use of so complex and allusive a style of writing. His response is oblique: he is working towards some sort of cultural patrimony (thus the reference to sleeping children with which *Laborintus II* ends) but points also to 'mud on the shoulders'. This in turn is a reference back to his polemical essay *Poesia informale* from the 'Novissimi' manifesto of 1961, where he spoke of the necessity of

throwing ourselves head-first into the labyrinth of irrationalism and formalism, indeed into a Palus Putredinis of anarchism and alienation, in the hope that ... having come through all that, we could emerge at the other side not just with dirty hands, but with mud all over our shoulders too.

Clearly, Berio also subscribed to the necessity of 'mud on the shoulders'. The texts of his major vocal works of the next five years, *Sinfonia* and *Opera*, all reflected the same heady brew. Yet with an instinctive sense of balance he matched verbal ellipsis and ambiguity with an increasingly direct musical idiom. In *Laborintus II* this is particularly striking. Three-part choirs of clarinets, trumpets, vibrato-less voices, trombones, and low strings echo each other, pursuing a harmonic discourse of great clarity and economy. Jazz is evoked at several points in the percussion parts, and by the ensemble and tape after the narrator has read fragments from the inscription over the gates of Hell. A maverick flute line, of the sort that had become Berio's trade-mark since the flute *Sequenza*, pursues its descants above the mêlée. Simple, trenchant gestures give the listener points of reference amidst the verbal labyrinth.

In *Sinfonia*, written three years later, he constructed his own labyrinth. The first and fifth movements in particular echo his previous work with Sanguineti. Here, however, the text was not a universally known classic, quotation from which would raise a rich fund of association in many listeners, but a recent and highly controversial work of structural anthropology—Claude Lévi-Strauss's *Le cru et le cuit*. This was the first of four books in which Lévi-Strauss set out to demonstrate structural analogies and transformations between myths from different tribes of South American Indians, often turning to Western musical forms and procedures to provide metaphors for the relations that he uncovered. Berio took a group of interrelated myths and in the main extracted fragments from Lévi-Strauss's commentary upon them. Projecting these into a typically complex vocal texture, he obliterated all perceptible links with the original framework, but liberated the poetic potential that lay dormant in Lévi-Strauss's tables and diagrams.

Such reduction of a large-scale borrowed structure to skeletal fragments was to find a musical parallel in the third movement of *Sinfonia*, whose commentary upon the scherzo from Mahler's Second Symphony was discussed in Chapter IV. But the principle text that Berio employed in this movement—Beckett's *The Unnameable*—has always resisted the attentions of structural analysts, sustaining itself, as it miraculously does, upon a barrage of ironic detail rather than upon any discernible narrative progression. So that in exploring Beckett's inferno (for that, in effect, is where this extraordinary monologue is located) Berio extracted such images as would serve to reflect musical events within the movement, or comment upon the ambiguities of concert-hall life. But where *Laborintus II* had ended with fragmentary allusions back to a discussion on the function of art, Berio ends this movement with an explicit equivalent. Setting aside Beckett for a moment, he expands upon a quotation from his own essay *Meditation on a Twelve-tone Horse* (1968), querying whether music might not indeed be able to change life and attempting an absurd declaration of faith. But this is instantly swept aside by Beckett's 'there must be something else. Otherwise it would be quite hopeless. But it is quite hopeless.' When paying homage to Joyce, Berio can draw music out of words. Here he reaches the other extreme, and lets words and music mark out the ineluctable distance that allows then to perform a mutual critique. It is the tension between them, rather than their apparent capacity for fusion, that provides the frame for his major theatrical works of the next two decades.

VI
DIGITAL SYSTEMS AND
FOLK-MUSIC

In 1971 Berio resigned his post at the Juilliard School. By now the burgeoning success of his music kept him in constant motion, and teaching became correspondingly difficult. Looking back, he commented rather ruefully that from 1970 to 1977 he spent his life in hotels. Perhaps it was by way of a counterbalance to this frenetic progress that he felt the need to re-establish a gravitational centre in Italy. So in 1972 he bought two adjacent farm buildings below Radicondoli, a hilltop village near Siena looking out over the valley of the Cecina, and began work restoring them and planting the land surrounding them with vineyards and fruit trees. By 1975 he was able to move in; and from 1977, when he married his third wife, the Israeli musicologist Talia Pecker, Radicondoli became a stable focus for his work. But from 1974 to 1980 a second focus was provided by Paris, where Boulez invited him to direct the electro-acoustic section of IRCAM.

Although Berio had included tape parts in *Laborintus II* (1965), *Questo vuol dire che* (1968–9), and *Opera* (1969–70), electronic resources now no longer played the central role in his work that they had from 1957 to 1961. To that extent, acceptance of Boulez's offer involved another return to long-established roots. Yet Berio's work at IRCAM did not immediately involve him in fresh creative ventures. Instead, he set to work supervising one of the Institute's more fruitful research projects. He invited the physicist, Peppino di Giugno, to devise a digital system that could overcome the principal impediment to a sophisticated use of live electronics: that of achieving a response from one's equipment so rapid that it is perceived as 'instantaneous', and thus allows the user the same interaction with other performers as is enjoyed by an instrumentalist or singer. If the various components of a complex system (say, oscillators, filters, etc.) are treated as a series of discrete 'black boxes' inputting and outputting into each other, such immediacy is hard to achieve. Di Giugno therefore broke down the functions necessary within each of these 'black boxes' into their basic components, and designed a system (the 4X) in which it was possible to program these according to the requirements of the individual work (and indeed of the environment in which it is to be performed). It gives a somewhat abstract notion of the 4X's scope to record that it can produce the equivalent of 1,024 simultaneous oscillators, or 450 second-order filters, or an extremely detailed sound analysis (a 4,096-point Fast Fourier Transform). Naturally, most works will instead require a combination of these functions, and the scope of each will be reduced accordingly. But for all that, di Giugno's system can be used to meet a formidable range of needs: synthesizing sounds, processing sounds produced by other performers, mixing sounds, and distributing them in space.

The attraction of the 4X for Berio was twofold. It permitted complex interaction between performers and electronics in 'real time', and thus relocated electronic music firmly in the realm of live performance. But it also allowed him to pursue in hugely magnified form a preoccupation that had its roots in his work in the *Studio di fonologia*. As was noted in Chapter II, one of the idiosyncrasies of the Milan studio was its use of a relatively large bank of oscillators to provide the basic materials for further manipulation. With the 4X he could contemplate the instantaneous generation and processing of huge banks of sound, which could then be fined down by filtering to achieve the desired result: a process known as subtractive synthesis.

Berio began a careful, but deliberately circumscribed exploration of the 4X's potential in 1979, and by 1980 had produced a *Chemins V* for clarinet and digital system from which, reversing his usual procedure, he then extracted *Sequenza IX* for clarinet alone. *Chemins V* took the process of commentary upon a solo line beyond the harmonic level, familiar from previous *Chemins*, to embrace the formant structure of clarinet sound itself. Berio's fascination with the interface between voice and instrument, so richly explored from *Circles* through to *Coro* (1975–6), here aimed for a utopic synthesis, for the sound of the clarinet was filtered with characteristics sampled from the vocal tract. Like a number of Berio's other experimental works, *Chemins V* was then withdrawn, but the *Sequenza* that he drew from it, with its melodic permutations within a slowly evolving pitch field, achieved rapid popularity.[1] Meanwhile Boulez took up the challenge of the 4X's capacities on a more substantial scale with his *Répons* (1980–81), where the system was used in combination with a large ensemble.

Berio resigned his post at IRCAM in 1980, but began negociations with the Commune of Florence with a view to setting up a research centre that could develop further some of the new perspectives suggested by his work in Paris. This was a protracted process, but one that finally bore fruit in 1987, when his new institute, Tempo Reale, began work in the Villa Strozzi. Tempo Reale means 'real time'. The choice of name has substantial resonances. It implies a commitment to active performance, to the unrepeatable here and now. (Technology, as manifested in the recording industry, has created a culture of the repeatable: here, at least, the tables are turned.)

The research group that Berio brought together at the Villa Strozzi began work on a new system, TRAILS, or Tempo Reale Audio Interactive Location System: 'interactive', because it allows its operator and the performers to respond to each other; 'location', because it is capable of placing and moving sounds in auditory space, indeed, of creating that space by suggesting an acoustic 'horizon' beyond the network of speakers by which listeners are surrounded. Once the positioning of those speakers within a given auditorium has been decided upon, the system is then programed to create its own 'architecture', as Berio defines it, and can thus make good the accoustic limitations of its environment, obliterating the traditional distinction between 'musical' and 'non-musical' spaces. Within that malleable architecture, TRAILS can process up to twenty-four simultaneous sound-events, and move them through up to eight different trajectories.

The dynamic possibilities opened up by these resources are echoed in the title of the first work in which Berio put them to use, *Ofanim* (1988), one of whose meanings in Hebrew is 'wheels'. It is a setting for two children's choirs, a female voice, and two instrumental groups, of two contrasting and interleaved Hebrew texts from the Old Testament: the apocalyptic vision of Ezekiel, and the sensual imagery of the Song of Songs. The hallucinatory dynamism of the four-faced creatures of Ezekiel 1, who come out of a whirlwind, move like lightning, and are 'as it were a wheel within a wheel' provides a verbal complement to the illusory spaces of the TRAILS system; the Song of Songs establishes the opposite pole, rooting the listener once more in the body. But Berio moves to a darker ending. Up to this point his female vocalist has remained silent, a crouching presence. As she slowly stands, the other performers fall silent. Her delivery of a text from Ezekial 19 casts a shadow over the celebration of the female body in the Song of Songs fragments, for here a mother is compared to a vine that at first is 'fruitful and full of branches', but is then uprooted in fury and cast to the ground. 'Now she is planted in the wilderness, in a dry and thirsty ground'. The image is a universal one, but it is Berio's intention that we should hear in it echoes of our own holocausts and exoduses, whether Hitler's Europe or America's Trail of Tears, today's Palestine or Stalin's Russia.

From the start, Berio's work at Tempo Reale emphasized practicality. Equipment developed there had to be well adapted for use in live performance, and relatively easy to transport and set up. (Despite its formidable technical achievements, the 4X had limitations on both counts.) More recent experimentation has therefore focused upon combining TRAILS with commercially available machines that can be used to program sound synthesis and processing on a smaller scale, with a view to making the components of a given timbre themselves mobile in space.

But even while Berio was fostering research in computer technology at IRCAM during the seventies, his own music was drawing increasingly upon what would appear to be a diametrically opposite source of stimulus: folk-song. This is perhaps only a superficial contradiction. Berio is entirely at home in Marshall McLuhan's post-telegraphic 'global village': although driven by an enduring empathy for folk-musics, his creative response to them sets its face against the cult of 'authenticity'. It may well be that, during this restless period of his career, the immediacy of music from traditional, 'closed' societies spoke to him with particular force. But he never allowed himself or his audiences any truck with escapist fantasies of noble savagery. His technical treatment of folk-models measured out the distance, however painful, between the traditional musician's direct and vivid response to his social environment, and the fluid, scattered identity offered to the contemporary western musician by an encyclopaedic range of stimuli and models.

Berio's visceral response to folk-music runs like a thread throughout his career. While a student at the Milan Conservatorio, he discovered Giuseppe Favara's anthologies of Sicilian folk-songs, and produced his own versions of two of the tunes that he found there in the *Due canti siciliani* of 1948. But admiration had already provoked 'exorcism' in the form of his own *Tre canzoni popolari* of 1946–7. He was to take up two of these, *La donna ideale* and *Ballo*, nearly twenty years later in what is perhaps his most frequently performed work, *Folk Songs* (1964). There they stand alongside other 'genuine' folk-melodies. The distinction is in the end only of modest relevance since, as Berio has commented, 'it is not my intention to preserve the authenticity of a folk song. My transcriptions are analyses'.[2]

From 1968 on, folk-musics began to play a more insistent role in Berio's work. Although he had not actively involved himself in ethnomusicological research, in that year he spent a month and a half in Sicily, and there recorded some of the *abbagnate*, or street vendors' songs. And in 1968–9 he put together a musical 'framework', entitled *Questo vuol dire che* (literally, 'This means that . . .'), into which a variety of events might be inserted from one performance to the next. The fixed frame of this piece united and developed on tape various examples of nasal folk-singing, mainly from Eastern Europe, while a vocal ensemble (originally the Swingle Singers) developed fragments from various regions of Italy, Croatia, Bulgaria, and Brittany. But although he was again to superpose recorded examples of folk-singing from widely divergent sources in a tape piece, *Chants parallèles*, written for French radio in 1974, in the main Berio avoided the direct quotation of folk-music in his music of the seventies. Instead, he used the technical resources of folk-melody as a starting-point for his own melodic invention.

The first, but vividly effective, step in this direction was taken in 1972 with *E vo'* for soprano and ensemble. This setting of the words of a Sicilian lullaby takes the form of a single arching expanse of melody whose details are clearly impregnated with Berio's study of southern Italian folk song. Slides, trills, and meticulously controlled dynamics take their place alongside the phonetic play discussed in the previous chapter to create an amalgam of striking conviction. Ex. VI.1 shows a phrase from the resultant vocal line.

If only because of its extended, arch-like structure, nobody could mistake *E vo'* for a folk-song. Yet that arch is built upon the familiar principle of gradually extending a fixed repertoire of focal notes. And it is just this feature of Berio's melodic praxis that he found reflected and amplified in his studies of folk-music, where a small selection of pitches are so often permutated to yield

Ex. VI.1 *E vo'*, vocal line only, 5–7

extraordinary melodic riches. He therefore found himself increasingly drawn to writing directly in a folk-song style. His first, light-hearted move in this direction came with *Cries of London* (1973), which although a latter-day version of the Renaissance conceit that integrated a medley of street cries into a madrigalian texture, was also in part inspired by his work on Sicilian *abbagnate*. Naturally, though, Sicilian idioms would not be at home in this context nor, with English traditions of street-singing long dead, was Berio tempted to play the antiquarian. So he simply compounded an imaginary folk-idiom, and set his texts accordingly.

This pleasant but minor *jeu d'esprit* would not be of great consequence were it not a clearing of the throat for the enterprise that followed. For from 1975 to 1977 Berio was at work on *Coro*, his major 'public' statement of the seventies, just as *Sinfonia* had been for the sixties. It was also his first attempt since *Sinfonia* to integrate voices and orchestra. But where in the earlier work he had relied upon amplification to achieve a balance between voices and instruments (and in some acoustics a capricious and delicate balance at that), in *Coro* he opted for a more radical solution. The chorus of the title refers to an ensemble of forty voices and forty melodic instruments, plus piano, electronic organ, and two percussionists. Each vocalist is associated with an instrumentalist, and the two are seated side by side so as to create a fully intregrated *tutti*. This can then be broken down to form the traditional chorus plus orchestra, a great variety of chamber ensembles, and duets from individual vocal-instrumental couples. The positioning of these couples on stage is in part dictated by grouping according to vocal tessitura, but is also designed so as to favour contrast and interplay between differing groups all over the stage—a revitalization of Berio's experiments with acoustic space from the late fifties.

Coro sets a mosaic of folk-texts, interleaved with fragments from Pablo Neruda's trilogy *Residencia en la Tierra* (1933–47).[3] The folk-texts come from a wide variety of sources. Those from North and South America, Polynesia and Africa are sung in a literal English translation which does not necessarily attempt to mould them according to the syntactic norms of their host language. Later sections of the work introduce Croatian texts sung in French, and Persian texts sung in German; but Italian dialect songs and a fragment from the Hebrew Song of Songs are both sung in their original languages. Again, Berio measures the distance between himself and his sources: only those with which he has an immediate relationship (in the case of the Hebrew through his third wife, Talia Pecker Berio) are set in their original form. The rest are distanced from their origins by translation, and from their new host language by nonconformity.

The choice of texts emphasizes basic experiences that in some measure transcend cultural distinctions: love, death, and work. But such human solidarity is placed in a more disquieting perspective by the Neruda fragments. These bridge one of the most significant developments within Neruda's work, juxtaposing the disturbing and subjective imagery of the 1933 *Residencia en la Tierra* and the populist and explicitly political idiom first explored in the *Tercera Residencia* of 1947. The 1933 collection is represented by the opening lines from *Débil del alba* and lines from near the close of *Colección nocturna*, each beginning with the words 'El dia'. *Débil del alba*, which comes to play so powerful a role in the final two sections of the work, depicts a desolate dawn, *Colección nocturna* dusk. The 1947 collection is represented by the final lines from *Explico algunas cosas*, a fierce denunciation of right-wing atrocities in the Spanish Civil War. But Berio sets aside the explicit accusation of Neruda's original ('Generales traidores: mirad mi casa muerta, mirad España rota'—Traitor generals: look at my dead house, look at broken Spain), and extracts a more generalized protest at the destruction of innocent lives. For much of the work he uses only the thrice-repeated final line: 'Venid a ver la sangre por las calles' (Come and see the blood in the streets), to which the *tutti* obsessively returns. Only at the very end do we discover that this is Neruda's answer to a hypothetical question: 'Preguntaréis por qué esta poesía no nos habla del sueño, de las hojas, de los grandes volcanes del país natal?' (You will ask why this poem doesn't tell us about dreams, leaves, the great volcanoes of my native land?). That same uncomfortable question about the borderline between art and ethics haunted both of Berio's other major works for voice(s) and orchestra—in the Brecht poem *An die Nachgeborenen* that brought down to earth the otherwise purely aesthetic revelations of *Epifanie*, and the Brecht-inspired quotation from his own essay *Meditation on a Twelve-Tone Horse* that invaded the end of the third movement of *Sinfonia*. And there are other echoes, for on consulting Neruda's poem we find that the 'blood in the streets' is that of children, killed in an air-raid—the same image that cut through and ended the machinations of *Opera* (see Chapter VII).

This darkening of the atmosphere, compounded by the use of *Debil del alba*, is eloquent testimony to the persistence with which Berio is drawn to use images of death as a necessary antithesis to the vitalistic aspects of his work; for *Coro* was originally intended simply as a celebration—a musical equivalent to the *Festival dell'Unità* to which Italy invites guests from many parts of the world. Only as he worked upon it did Berio come to accentuate the perennial threat to the basic human values of love and work. Within this perspective, *Coro* had to end, as Berio himself said, with a question mark.[4] That alertness to the vulnerability of humanistic values is still urgently present in *Ofanim*, discussed above, but it reached its fiercest and most devastating expression in *La vera storia* (see Chapter VII), upon which Berio started work soon after he had completed *Coro*.

Although using folk-texts, however transmogrified by translation, Berio employs no analogous procedures in his music: only one piece of original folk-material is quoted, a Macedonian tune that makes a fleeting appearance in section V. Returning for a moment to McLuhan, if the world network of electronic information may be seen as an extension of the human nervous system, then in *Coro* Berio takes this vision to its logical conclusion. For Berio's 'global village' is not merely one of external, technological fact, but of internal, psychological possibility. The fragments of other cultures that make up each individual's sense of the 'world' can be used anecdotally, momentarily reassuring us that we know who we are by telling us what we are not. But equally, they can be set interacting and cross-fertilizing: a process that ultimately compels us to recognize the sense of identity that comes from 'belonging' as a paradise to be resolutely, perhaps indeed cheerfully lost.

The spirit of this project can be typified through a technical feature that plays an important role within the larger architecture of *Coro*. At the time of writing *Coro*, Berio had fresh in his mind a remarkable study by the Israeli ethnomusicologist Simha Arom of the wooden-trumpet bands of the Central African Republic.[5] Within these bands, each instrument plays a single note in a complex, but apparently independent rhythmic pattern. The result might suggest to Western listeners a jubilant anarchy devoid of any common metric basis. But by recording each performer separately, superposing the results, and thereby re-creating precisely the same 'anarchic' structure as he had originally recorded when all the musicians were playing together, Arom was able to demonstrate the existence of an unsounded central line, against which each player was performing his own elaborate rhythmic counterpoint. Berio did not attempt a straightforward recreation: after all, unsounded central lines, provided by the conductor, are the stock in trade of orchestral rhythm in the music of the fifties and sixties. Instead, he established a clear common-time semiquaver pulse, and assigned to each brass instrument a single note (in the case of trombones, two) and its own pattern of semiquaver attacks. The result sounded as close to a fourteenth-century European hocket as to a Central African trumpet band. The first appearance of this texture, in section IX, typifies the hybrids that proliferate within Berio's global village, for there it articulates the melodic contour of a Macedonian tune (though not the same one as was quoted in Section V) as a setting of a text from the Gabon.

The sheer variety of resources, punctuated by the vast block chords characteristic of the Neruda sections, gives *Coro* a mosaic-like surface. But beneath it Berio is careful to co-ordinate a satisfying large-scale framework. The first eight sections establish a pattern of folk-settings, in which individual voices predominate, alternating with brief *tutti* settings of Neruda. The last of these is, however, more extended; it is also the first to combine a fragment from the 1933 collection with the ubiquitous 'venid a ver . . .'. In the next eight sections (IX–XVI) voices in ensemble predominate. The hocket technique discussed above appears for the first time during IX, and is developed extensively in XI. These again alternate with 'venid a ver . . .', a pattern continued by the solo sections XIII and XV. XVI should thus once more be a Neruda setting, but for the first time the alternating pattern is broken. Instead the Sioux text used at the opening of the work returns, now set to the hocket textures established in this section.

Although this synthesis rounds off the first half of the work, Berio does not make of it an exaggerated climax that would underline the work's symmetries too forcefully. Even so, the second half of *Coro* mirrors the structure of the first. The next group of eight sections (XVII–XXIV) is pre-eminently for solo voices: the orchestral *tutti* makes one substantial intervention at XX, the upper half of the choral *tutti* at XI. It also marks a proliferation of languages (heralded in XV, where a German translation of a Persian text breaks the regular alternation between English and Spanish). In XVII, XXII, and XXIII French translations of Croation texts are used; and in the final section of this group, XXIV, Italian, German, and English combine: the first multilingual mix in the work. In the final group of seven sections (XXV–XXXI) massed forces predominate (broken only by the Hebrew setting, XXIX), and the multilingual mix continues. The structural parallel with the first half is emphasized by immediately reintroducing the hocket technique (XXV), and then gradually transforming it into something less ebullient and more disquieting. It thus helps to establish the 'alrededor de llanto' (environment of lament) that permeates the final sections of *Coro*.

The handling of dense harmonic aggregates when writing for massed forces in *Coro* shows many parallels with previous large-scale works. But the solo melodies emphasize the intense interest in generating abundance from limited resources that Berio had developed from his study of folk-musics. To show this well, one would need to quote at length. But a single example from section XIII may serve to give at least the flavour of the enterprise. This section is a setting of a Peruvian text for a series of tenor soloists, each accompanied by a cello. At first the vocal lines receive heterophonic commentary from oboe or cor anglais. Meanwhile, flutter-tongue flutes, muted violas, electronic organ, and percussion provide a sustained backdrop. Tenor 7 starts the section with only two notes, F♯ and G. After seven bars he admits two more, C♯ and G; and in his final flourish adds a B♭. Tenor 10 enters, as in Ex. VI.2, to develop this pitch repertoire, after which Tenor 9 expands it yet further. In responding to the vocal line, the double reeds—in Ex. VI.2 a cor anglais—use a broader version

Ex. VI.2 *Coro*, XIII, reduction of bars 18–25

Ex. VI.2 *(cont.)*:

of the same fixed field. By contrast, the accompanying cellos provide an increasingly animated counterpoint that is quite independent of the voice's pitches. (Missing from the reduction in Ex. VI.2 are the quiet gong strokes that mark the start of each bar.)[6]

These simple, folk-like vocal lines were to reach their most fluid, and most trenchantly expressive form in some of the *Ballate* from Act I of *La vera storia*, to be discussed in the next chapter. But they represent only one pole of Berio's response to popular melody. Just as earlier in the seventies he had followed the direct appeal of the *Concerto* for two pianos with the technical concentration of *Eindrücke*, so now *Coro* was followed by *Ritorno degli snovidenia* (1977) for solo cello and small orchestra. This is yet another work where a central line engenders a fluid and subtle harmonic commentary. But the nature of that central line is altogether different from the abstract wave-forms of *Bewegung* or *Points on the Curve to Find*.... Since Berio was writing *Ritorno degli snovidenia* for the Russian cellist Rostropovich, he took as his starting-point three fragments from Russian revolutionary songs. These provided Berio with characteristic inflections and gestures, to be incorporated within a constantly self-regenerating stream of melody—an enormously expanded version of the process at work in *E vo*.

Snovidenia is the Russian for 'dreams': Berio's title therefore means 'return of the dreams'. On a poetic level, the title implies a

86

homage to the dreams of the Russian revolution, betrayed by history but still returning to haunt the imagination. Yet *Ritorno* also marks a return within the context of Berio's own work, a rediscovery of his most richly imaginative melodic vein. Even the details of that melody echo the same theme, for unlike, say, *Sequenza I* or *Sequenza VII*, the melodic writing here is emphatically motivic. The gesture of two rapid upbeats a tone apart ushering in a longer note on the intervening semitone recurs constantly, and yet generates extraordinary melodic variety.

The ebb and flow of that melody over a three and a half octave range is distinctively conditioned by the harmonic backdrop that it generates. In the later stages of *O King* certain of the notes from the pitch set are sustained as a harmonic backdrop from one appearance of the note in the melodic line to the next. This principle is much expanded in *Ritorno*, and creates a peculiarly close-knit interdependence between melody and harmonic backdrop. Despite covering an enormous range, the melody must perforce tend to return to any pitch area that it has recently touched upon. But this is not the circumscribed pitch set of *O King*, nor the slowly evolving pitch field of *Bewegung*. The self-regenerating variety of the melodic line therefore produces an extremely rich and constantly shifting harmonic palette. The gradual conquest of harmonic abundance that had come to the surface in an intuitive, exploratory way in a work such as *Sequenza IV*, and been pursued methodically through the quieter, more austere works of the early seventies, here found its richest vindication to date.

Because he had so fully absorbed the example of folk-song into his own composition, Berio was now ready to enter into a new, and more direct contract with such materials, but in a new way. In *Voci* (1984), he placed transcriptions of Sicilian folk-songs as performed by the Sicilian viola player, Aldo Bennici, within so fluid and responsive a framework that any sense of quotation is dissolved. Berio subtitled *Voci* 'Folk Songs II', but the work shows none of the clear distinctions between folk-melody and concert-hall commentary that lent piquancy to *Folk Songs*. (Typically, he then challenged this synthesis in *Naturale* (1985–6) by combining materials developed from *Voci* with his own 1968 recordings of the Sicilian *abbagnate* singer Celano: a confrontation of the raw and the cooked.)

Voci underlines two other aspects of Berio's work in the

seventies and eighties. Firstly, like *Coro*, it maps out a distinctive aural space. It is written for two ensembles: a central nucleus clustered around the solo viola, and a semicircular line of players surrounding them at a distance, and providing an acoustic perimeter. Around that perimeter, registral regions are distinguished spatially: bass instruments sit at the front on either side, isolated from other medium-range groups towards the back by violins and high woodwind. This emphasis upon acoustic space runs through much of Berio's recent work. He employs a similar conception for *Concerto II (Echoing Curves)* (1988–9), where the solo pianist is surrounded by an inner ensemble, in turn surrounded by the rest of the orchestra–an arrangement that recalls the first version of *Chemins III*, discussed in Chapter IV. And as in *Chemins III*, the spatial disposition emphasizes the fact that a pre-existent work, here *Points on the Curve to Find . . .*, is embedded within the new one.

Formazioni (1985–7) articulates a more complex spatial conception. Berio rearranges his orchestra so as to place a group of clarinets and a double bassoon at the centre, surrounded by strings with the bass instruments brought to the front. Around this central core, wind groups are placed so as to facilitate spatial dialogue: brass groups on raised platforms pass chord formations to and fro between extreme left and extreme right. Flutes from woodwind groups at front left and back right initiate a duet across the central body of strings. But it is in the tutti sections that these forces come into their own. At first, the work is anchored around a central *E*, from which harmonic formations splay out on either side. As these formations gradually break loose, and textures grow denser, Berio distinguishes the concurrent layers of musical activity by their different trajectories around the ensemble.

All of these works give fresh impetus to Berio's spatial experiments of the fifties (which had been kept alive in the intervening period by the first version of *Chemins III*, and *Ora* (1971), both subsequently withdrawn). The TRAILS project discussed above is clearly a more articulated expression of the same concerns. In every instance, the listener's sharpened awareness of acoustic space underlines their own place within it. Being made physically self-aware by sound is in effect an invitation to act: to listen alertly and interrogatively.

For any musician with a measure of practical craftsmanship, that interrogation may extend beyond listening: *Voci* is itself the end result of such a process. Berio's interest in initiating a dialogue with other people's musical propositions has grown stronger in recent years. Some of his responses take the form of transcriptions, others are more complex. Even in the sixties, when arranging songs for a recital that Cathy Berberian gave at the 1967 Venice Biennale, he was exploring a range of possibilities: Kurt Weill he simply re-instrumentated, but Paul McCartney and John Lennon were subjected to what he described in the programme as a 'stylistic test' that involved transplanting their melodies to a neo-baroque environment. In 1975, bemused to discover that Boccherini had produced four different versions of his *La ritirata notturna di Madrid* (a descriptive piece evoking the tattoo that recalls soldiers to their quarters), Berio proceded to superpose them, and to subject the result to a decidedly modern orchestration. Yet three years later he was orchestrating de Falla's *Siete canciones populares españolas* in a spirit of absolute fidelity to the composer's own orchestral sound. That capacity for recreating another man's orchestra has been exercised in even more startling form in recent years, in his versions of Brahms's Clarinet Sonata, Op. 120 No. 1, (1986), with its subtle compensations for the pedal effects of the original, and of Mahler's early songs (1986–7). But he has also formulated his own response to (and critique of) a major musicological temptation: that of completing unfinished works. In *Rendering* (1988–9), rather than attempt to fill out the fragmentary sketches that Schubert left for his Tenth Symphony, Berio treats them rather as one might a damaged fresco, and fills the gaps with material that makes no attempt at completion (although it, too, is derived from Schubert, notably the last piano sonata and the 'Wanderer' Fantasy), and announces its alien nature by the non-Schubertian sound of the celesta. Such dialogues are continuing testimony to Berio's refusal to be bound by the polarized roles of contemporary musical life. His father trained him to be a musician at large, and he demands of his audiences that they should cultivate similarly generous aspirations.

VII
BERIO'S THEATRE

During the seventies and eighties stage works have assumed a central role within Berio's output. In one sense these transpose into the opera house a theatre of the imagination whose essential features he had established long before. His awareness of a purely musical dramaturgy had been profoundly influenced, as a student, by the discovery of Monteverdi's madrigals, to which Ghedini made frequent reference in his composition classes. His eight years of work for Milan radio had added to this a sharp sense of the extraordinary flexibility of the aural imagination, where images can flow into, or coexist with one another with an ease denied to the eye. By the end of the fifties, he was consciously conceiving of a purely instrumental work such as *Différences* (1959) in terms of an implicit, abstract dramaturgy, but could also plan an explicit, though wordless theatre of vocal and electronic gesture in *Visage* (1960–1). Both share in the vivid, gestural quality, discussed in Chapter III, that permeates his work through to the early seventies.

The notion of 'gesture' implies an imaginary physicality. The history of European music abounds with music derived from dance that is to be listened to, not acted upon, and that cultivates ideals of motion and gesture only imperfectly realized in the real world. (Berio himself provided a mordant potted history of one instance of this, the frenetic sensual phantasies surrounding the concert-hall waltz, in his conflations of Mahler, Berlioz, Strauss, and Ravel in *Sinfonia*.) Berio's own gestural world of the fifties and sixties was often violent and nervous, exploiting music's command of an imaginary physicality beyond the disciplines of dance. This, combined with his complex exploration of voices and words made for a theatre of the ear so potent, that its importation on to the real stage was possible only when a certain visual sobriety was observed. Thus *Passaggio* demands a single woman crossing the stage, and stopping at different points to sing. But it is the tension between the highly subjective fragments of phantasy and memory sung from the stage, and the responses of groups in the auditorium 'speaking for' the audience that create the dramatic substance of the piece: the visual component is simply an adjunct to a theatre of the mind. Indeed, in *Laborintus II*, the visual component is optional and unspecified. By contrast, the balance between visual and aural components that Berio was to achieve in his major theatrical works of the seventies and eighties was reached by disciplining the gestural urgency of the idiom that he developed during the sixties into a melodic and harmonic continuity that could knit together the multiplicity of visual events and verbal imagery that his sense of the 'open work' demanded.

From the start, Berio's theatrical priorities were clear. As was noted in Chapter II, his first experiment with tape music had been called *Mimusique No. 1* (1953). In the same year he completed an orchestral score, *Mimusique No. 2* that similarly evoked gestural situations without following an explicit scenario. But in 1955 came the opportunity to provide a short theatrical piece for the 'Teatro delle Novità' Festival at Bergamo. Berio therefore asked Roberto Leydi to write a scenario that would fit around *Mimusique No. 2*, and once the outlines were established, revised and extended his score, adding a 'Rhumba-ramble'. Leydi took his inspiration from the 'palliatives' against the harshnesses of life that Freud had listed in *Civilization and its Discontents*, and put together a didactic scenario of a vaguely Brechtian cut,[1] *Tre modi per sopportare la vita* (to whose straightforward ironies and finale in praise of 'solidarity' the first-night audience at Bergamo in 1955 reacted with vigorous invitations to the authors to leave for Russia immediately). But even at this stage Berio's sense of theatre was evident. He resisted the new-found complexities of his works for the concert hall (or in the case of the 'Rhumba-ramble' used them with a dry wit that belies their elevated origins) and kept to a simple, graphic idiom that would not overturn the delicate balance between visual and aural input.

Berio's work of the late fifties evidently continued to suggest to his contemporaries a theatre of gesture, for when he received a commission from the 1959 Venice Biennale, it was once again for a mime piece. As his work list shows, this was a period of intensive production, so it is perhaps not surprising that he decided to use the opportunity to rework within a more satisfactory context materials from his earlier theatrical venture. This time, he turned to his friend and fellow-Ligurian Italo Calvino to provide him with a scenario. Calvino responded with a typically oblique narrative. The new work was to be entitled *Allez Hop*: the cry of the travelling showman as he puts his performing fleas to work. Unfortunately, one of the fleas gets loose, and reduces the complacent stability of human society to mayhem with a few swift jumps and bites. Eventually order is restored, and with it complacency. The showman takes stock of the situation, opens the door of the fleas' cage, and walks away.

This anarchic demonstration of the primacy of the body was the last fully fledged story that Berio was ever to tell on stage. His next theatrical venture, *Passaggio* (1962), established the foundations for a form of musical theatre that he has continued to develop to this day, in which narrative provides at best no more than a skeletal framework for a proliferating network of verbal and visual images. Berio's initial plan for this work centred around the image of a woman slowly crossing the stage, and stopping from time to time to sing. Her texts would echo those passages in Kafka's *Letters to Milena* where he describes his feelings at being compelled, for lack of anywhere more private, to meet her in a public garden in Vienna. When Sanguineti joined him in the project, he began to expand upon Berio's idea, introducing materials suggested by Rosa Luxembourg's prison diaries. The project rapidly developed its own momentum, and although the result, *Passaggio*, bears traces of both these sources, they are no more than strands within a complex and innovative whole.

All of Berio's vocal works from this period derive their dynamism from a polarized creative framework. In *Circles*, that framework had been provided by the tension between language as sense and as sound. Here it is even more overt, for it arises from the disposition of his vocal forces, and the roles assigned to them. On stage is a single female protagonist. In the orchestra pit is a substantial ensemble (predominantly of wind and percussion) and an eight-part choir that comments on the action from different standpoints.[2] Spaced around the auditorium are five groups of speakers who give brutally self-revealing voice to the inner thoughts of a cultured, bourgeois audience.

The nameless female protagonist (described simply as 'She' in the score) moves through a series of 'stations', so named in ironic parallel to the Stations of the Cross, and indeed furnished by Sanguineti with quotations from the Vulgate by way of titles.

'She' is discovered flattened against the back of the stage in Station I, is seated beneath a cone of violent light in Station III, is seen behind bars in Station IV, and in a shabby urban bed-sit in Station V. From these visual cues, and from the reactions of the two choruses we infer a story of arrest, interrogation, and subsequent freedom. After a reflective choral epilogue (see Ex. III.7), the singer reappears. 'She' has done with acting and is putting on her raincoat to go home, but revisits the various Stations, and sings of a search at II, interrogation at III, being forced to sign a statement at IV, and being told that there is a room where she can sleep at V. Then, in a gesture borowed from Genet's *Le Balcon*, she turns on the audience and tells them to get out: the speaking chorus leads the audience in applause. Although this final station confirms a skeletal narrative structure, 'She' reacts to it only sporadically (notably in IV where, in the midst of jumbled Latin fragments from Lucretius, she protests that she does not want liberty since prison at least confers an identity upon her). But otherwise she appears to be absorbed in a stream of recollections and confused reactions: images of search and sexual arousal lapsing into absurdity in II, a garden idyll that turns to nightmare while the chorus in the pit sings of torture in III, and a search round her room in V, pulling out of trunks and wardrobes a tangled jumble of possessions.

The speaking groups in the audience provide a devastating counterpoint. Taking up the polyglot idiom of Sanguineti's poetry, they voice their comments in a simultaneous barrage of Italian, French, English, German, and in their more incantatory moments of self-contemplation, Latin. They invoke social order, abuse and lust after the protagonist (as she is tortured, they chant 'kein ende' again and again), pray that they may be saved from the wrath of the poor, auction a 'perfectly domesticated woman', and recite lists of consumer goods that turn into a horrifying catalogue of weapons (while 'She' lies down on her bed and starts to strip).

Evidently the authors were in some measure looking for trouble, and their first-night audience at the Piccola Scala did not disappoint them. But as the more vocal members of the audience began to protest at finding themselves under attack from their own side of the proscenium, they heard their exclamations echoed and transformed by the speaking chorus, whom Berio had instructed to improvise in this fashion whenever appropriate. With their favourite weapon neutralized, or rather absorbed into the piece, the Milanese audience was compelled to endure the authors' barbs as best they might. (Subsequent audiences came forewarned, and did not repeat the furore.)

This 'messa in scena' (a punning description, meaning both 'put on stage' and 'mass on stage') contains in concentrated form many of the most crucial elements of Berio's theatre. Its superimposed layers of verbal material oblige listeners to find their own paths through the aural jungle, and to embrace that singular mixture of aesthetic alertness and receptiveness that springs from the half understood. But while the logocentric part of the mind is learning to live with insecurity, the ear is focused by a music of visceral directness. *Passaggio* deliberately avoids the sophistications of a work for the concert hall such as *Epifanie*. Instead, it traces a rapid, mosic-like 'passage' between vividly contrasted textures and musical procedures.

Such living in the present was entirely appropriate for a short, and clearly sectional theatre-piece like *Passaggio*. It proved more problematic in the entirely non-narrative *Esposizione*, upon which Berio and Sanguineti were working for the Venice Biennale of 1963. Again, the backbone of this piece was movement. But where in *Passaggio* the implications of a seated audience watching a woman move on a stage were explored in psychological and ideological depth, here the relationship between static audience and highly mobile actor/dancers was less acutely focused. Ann Halprin's troupe started from the back of the auditorium, and progressively invaded the whole theatrical space, bringing with them a vast clutter of the objects by possession of which we define our 'selves'. Climbing-nets were suspended from the proscenium, by means of which the dancers and their baggage occupied the vertical dimension (notably, La Fenice's boxes). Finally, they all disappeared at the back of the stage. Sanguineti's texts were introduced sporadically, piling up parallel lists of cultural clutter.

Only when the verbal and musical materials of *Esposizione* were reworked in *Laborintus II* did they find a more cogent and compelling form. With the introduction of Dante as a focal point, and particularly Dante's critique of usury, around which Sanguineti could articulate images of rampant aquisitiveness, the work aquired a centre of gravity. But it also became pre-eminently a theatre of the imagination, complete in itself (and indeed first presented as a radio broadcast, although in this version quotations from Dante were rather thicker on the ground). Its trenchantly direct idiom has attracted a number of theatrical productions, but the problem of what cogently to add to so rich a mix has not been easily solved.

If a spatial process proved insufficient to articulate a large-scale theatrical form in *Esposizione*, the solution was soon to fall into Berio's hands, for the concert-hall pieces of the later sixties focused increasingly upon musical process. On a small scale, this is clear enough from *Sequenza VII* for oboe (1969) (see Ex. III.5). But more crucial to the large-scale perspectives required by music theatre was his work, in 1969, on the last movement of *Sinfonia*. This draws together the diverse materials of previous movements and explores ways of making them interact. The first movement of *Sinfonia* ends just as a solo piano has established itself in opposition to the orchestra, but its materials are left in suspended animation by the closing chords of the movement. They are only released to develop further at the start of the last movement where they lead into the central pitch line of the second movement, *O King*. This in turn sparks off associations with other movements as it procedes. These two principles, the interruption and later resumption of processes, and the reworking of familiar material within new contexts, between them provided the frame for Berio's next major project, his first full-length theatre-work, *Opera* (1970).

Opera occupies a singular place within Berio's output. It is his most complex experiment with 'open' musical theatre. But its experimental density was its downfall: the first production at Santa Fe was, as Berio readily admits, a fiasco, and subsequent European performances of a revised version, though receiving a more sympathetic reception, have failed to establish the work as a convincing entity. Yet for anyone wishing to understand the development of Berio's music theatre in the late seventies and eighties, *Opera* is an essential point of reference. The last movement of *Sinfonia* had set up interactions between three very different musico—verbal projects (commentaries upon Lévi-Strauss, *O King*, and Mahler). *Opera*, by contrast, was built around the relations between three contrasted layers of dramatic material that are united by a common theme. All three are narrations about death. The first consists of fragments from Striggio's libretto for Monteverdi's *Orfeo*. The second offers a sardonic dramatized documentary about the sinking of the Titanic—the remnant of a project conceived in 1956 by Umberto

Eco, Furio Colombo, and Berio as a parable upon the vulnerability of man's trust in technical perfection. The third derives from a then current production by Jo Chakin's Open Theatre of New York, *Terminal*, that pilloried our treatment of the dying. (In this respect, too, *Opera* echoes *Sinfonia*, where death is the theme that links all the movements together, albeit in a rather less emphatic way.) These three layers are so arranged that each constantly alludes to, or dissolves into, the other.

There is thus no narrative, simply a dream-like ebb and flow of interacting materials. (Eco's texts from the Titanic project revolve around isolated images or retrospective fragments.) But Berio provides one important concession to the expectations aroused by a proscenium arch: a denouement. The oneiric theatre of the mind that Berio has projected on to the stage is interrupted by the direct representation of death: that of two panic-stricken children, hunted down by searchlights. Voices from the pit sing an *Agnus Dei*; the mezzo-soprano slowly enters, picks up one of the children's dolls, and cradling it in her arms sings the lullaby *E vo'* as a valedictory lament. The materials from *Terminal* and the Titanic project are presented with Brechtian detachment, but this ending breaks through to command an immediate empathy.

If a sense of ending is achieved by dramatic means, structure is otherwise achieved by musical ones. The score consists of a series of separate numbers (some of them autonomous pieces that can be performed independently of *Opera*: Berio conceives of the title as the plural of 'opus'), and the patterns created by them form the basis of the large-scale structure. The first three numbers of the first Act are crucial in this respect. The work opens with *Air I*: a soprano is seen on stage learning the aria (setting an English translation of the prologue to Striggio's *Orfeo*) with a pianist. Then follows *Concerto I*, a substantial and complex piece, built, as so often in Berio's music, from a counterpoint of different layers of material, some of which is derived from *Tempi Concertati*. Thirdly, *Memoria*, a setting for baritone of the messenger's text from Striggio's *Orfeo*. Three other numbers complete the first Act (the last of them, *Tracce*, presumably a survivor from *Traces*). Act II starts with *Air II*—this time a more secure and elaborated version with first a flute and then strings joining in. It is followed immediately by a reworking of *Memoria*. Again, a series of other numbers follow. The third Act ties up these threads. It starts with *Air III*: a final and complete performance, though one to which other layers are gradually added, then the final version of *Memoria*, which is followed immediately by the most extensive and ambitious piece in the work, *Concerto II*. This picks up, and richly develops, the materials of *Concerto I* (though at a certain point the piano starts to work in materials from *Air* as well). *Concerto II* leads straight into the denouement discussed above.

Autonomous musical items in *Opera* such as *Air* or *E vo'* (see Ex. VI.1) allow Berio a wide-ranging melodic invention. But apart from the relative density of the two *Concerti*, he tends to maintain a spare, direct idiom that will not mask the abundant spoken material nor detract from events on stage. Even so there are problems. *Opera* contains more speech than do any of Berio's other theatrical works: most of the Titanic and *Terminal* materials are recited over an orchestral accompaniment. Actors are consequently compelled to shout for much of the time, and tend to compete for attention with the musical substance of *Concerto I*, which has an important role within the large-scale musical framework. Indeed, the fascination with torrents of speech spills over into one of the odder autonomous numbers, *Melodrama*. Here a nervous middle-aged tenor, who is plainly having trouble with his top G, talks himself into giving a perfomance of a Heine setting via a remorseless barrage of Anglo-American clichés whose main fascination to Berio was plainly their alliterative qualities (' "Big boy," I said, "I'm turning the tables on *you*. You blew the bit and now you'll have to bite the bullet" ', etc.). But perform he eventually does, and indeed sails triumphantly up to a high A before falling away to a close. (This modest study of performance neuroses prefigures a more extended essay on the same topic, *Recital*, written for Cathy Berberian in 1972.)

The overall musico-dramatic shape that emerges in *Opera* is a progress from maximal diversity of resources in Acts I and II, to the richer musical concentration of Act III. In a more sophisticated and carefully controlled form this process was to underpin Berio's two later full-scale music theatre works. But in the seven-year gap that separated the disconcerting failure of *Opera*, and the start of work on *La vera storia* he had set himself to explore the more explicit methods of harmonic control discussed in Chapter IV. These allowed him to bring closer to the surface the underlying continuities that he had begun to explore in *Opera*, and in so doing enormously to strengthen the cumulative impact of his musico-dramatic structure. Whether *Opera* is experienced as more than

97

the sum of its parts is an open question; but *La vera storia* is a single entity whose various components only take on a full significance within the context of the whole.

The experimental years of the early and mid-seventies were not completely devoid of musico-dramatic work, for Berio returned to the medium with which he had long been associated in his 'radio documentary' *A-Ronne* of 1974, and the radio work *Diario immaginario* (based upon Molière's *Le Malade imaginaire*) of 1975. *A-Ronne* in particular showed the continuing vitality of Berio's 'theatre of the imagination', based as it was upon multiple explorations of a short poem by Sanguineti that treats of 'beginnings' and 'ends' (in the body and beyond). The original version profited greatly from the imagination and vitality of the five actors with whom Berio created the work at Radio Hilversum, generating between themselves a series of fragmentary dramas teased by Berio from the text (an improvisational process not unlike that with which Berio and Berberian created the basic materials for *Visage*, discussed in Chapter III). Having put together the work on tape, Berio then reworked it in the following year as a concert piece scored for his usual eight-voice ensemble.[3]

The genesis of *La vera storia*, upon which Berio worked with Italo Calvino from 1977 to 1981, illustrates Berio's approach to musical theatre with some clarity. Berio started with his own conception of the musico-dramatic framework. The whole work was to grow from the pitch field established in its opening pages—so much so, that he once described the work as a 'passacaglia' (a metaphor that should not be taken too literally, however). With a clear sense of the overall dramatic shape in his mind, he was able to work quite extensively on the development of his musical materials before he approached Italo Calvino to fine down that dramatic shape into concrete poetic images. For Calvino, the technical challenge of fitting images to a pre-ordained musico-dramatic process, indeed often to pre-composed music, was both novel and stimulating (though naturally it carried with it echoes of the simpler task that he had faced twenty years before with *Allez-Hop*). But the result of this unusual procedure was a work of remarkable cohesion.

La vera storia divides into two parts. The first of these, like *Opera*, interleaves three different levels, though here they are much more richly interdependent dramatically, and clearly distinct musically: alternations between them map out a lucid musico-dramatic form. The structural corner-stones around which Part I is constructed are four large choruses which develop the image of the *festa*, or popular feast-day. These were the starting-point of the collaboration between Berio and Calvino. In a note on the libretto, Calvino underlined the importance to twentieth-century anthropology of the notion of the feast as 'a temporal discontinuity, where transgression takes the place of the norm, where the squandering of energies and goods takes the place of economic logic, to the point of sacrifice, the immolation of victims, destruction.'[4]

The *festa* sections of Part I thus continue the concern with collective well-being (and the threat posed to it by authoritarian repression) that had echoed through the Neruda sections from Berio's previous large-scale work, *Coro*. But here the crowd is viewed in all its ambivalence. The *Prima Festa*, which opens the work, establishes the anarchic energy and all-inclusiveness of the *festa* with a motto that is to run through the whole of *La vera storia*: 'nella festa tutto' (in the *festa*, everything). But it also introduces images of brutality and sacrifice: and as it finishes, a condemned man is led in to be executed by firing-squad. As he composes his thoughts in the face of death, the chorus comment with a mixture of sadistic glee and pity, and after the execution explode into the *Seconda Festa*, where they finally resolve upon rebellion. Later in Part I, in the *Terza Festa*, insurrection does indeed break out, but is brutally suppressed by the police. Compelled to acknowledge defeat, in the *Quarta Festa* the crowd resign themselves to taking up 'the long wait' once more. These sections share a feature common to all three of Berio's mature theatre works, in that they offer the director a chance to organize an abundance of simultaneous events: the visual equivalent to the semantic labyrinths of *Passaggio* or *Sinfonia*.

Berio's theatre learnt from Brecht the necessity for a constant interplay between losing oneself in the spectacle, and being conscious of oneself as spectator. So in *La vera storia* he used the four *festa* sections as a frame within which to scrutinize the conventions of nineteenth-century opera—the repertoire that forms the *raison d'être* of the building in which the work is to be performed—with an eye trained by the dispassionate tradition of structuralist criticism. The nineteenth-century librettist's art consisted in fleshing out a restricted range of dramatic situations and musical forms in a seemingly inexhaustible variety of historical, geographical, and psychological local colour. Part I of *La vera storia* follows through a string of these archetypical situations in all their nakedness. The protagonists who create them have names (a luxury to be withheld in the second part) and the few elemental characteristics necessary to create interaction, but no more. (The conception clearly owes a good deal to the 'skeletal' narrative of *Passaggio*). There are strong echoes of Cammarano's gloriously improbable libretto for Verdi's *Il Trovatore*—it is surely no accident that Berio chose as his model the Verdi opera that most severely taxes a sophisticated audience's capacity to suspend disbelief—but because each situation is reduced to its dramatic kernel Berio is able, like Verdi before him, to treat it entirely seriously.

The action stems from the execution by firing-squad that follows on from the *Prima Festa*. Ada, 'perhaps the daughter of the condemned man', steals the baby son of Ugo, the governor of the city. Consumed by grief, Ugo collapses and dies, while his eldest son, Ivo, swears vengeance in the form of general reprisals. Ivo and his younger brother, Luca, are rivals for the love of Leonora. They fight (represented by two dancers); Ivo is wounded, and throws Luca into prison. Luca now personifies resistance to repression: Ada and Leonora agonize over his fate. Luca is led towards a firing-squad, but at this point any concern with individuals and their fate dissolves into the collective resignation of the *Quarta Festa*. Ada then advances to the front of the stage to remind the audience that in the face of suffering and injustice one thing at least is possible: to refuse to forget it.

Each of these situations is embodied in a separate number with its own title, and distinct textual and musical character. Although, as Calvino noted, 'the gamut of sentiments is that of the nineteenth-century lyrical theatre (justice and oppression, generosity and vengeance, amorous devotion and jealousy, liberty and prison)', his protagonists are more or less free from the obligations of narrative detail. Each gives voice to a cluster of poetic images: and the more passive the protagonist, the more wide-ranging the scope of his or her text. Leonora, in effect no more than the passive object of others' passion, is assigned the richest range of imagery and the most complex and taxing vocal line. By contrast Ada, in constant interraction with her environment, is given words of incisive immediacy, and an urgently expressive idiom.

A third level, one of often ironic commentary, is provided by popular songs sung by *cantastorie*. Berio had long been fascinated by the art of Sicilian ballad-singers, or *cantastorie*—indeed, the title of *La vera storia* derives from the *cantastorie*'s opening gambit 'I'll tell you the true story of . . .' (though lovers of *Il Trovatore* will not have forgotten that, at the start of the opera, the chorus ask Ferrando to tell them '*la vera storia . . . di Garcia*'). The six ballads that Berio intersperses throughout Part I are not all derived from folk-song idioms: some of them are closer to the urban popular music of the mass media, and are accordingly acompanied in one instance by two guitars, in another by a pianola. But their contribution to the architecture of Part I lies in the extraordinary intensity of the final two ballads: '*Che il canto faccia un lungo viaggio*' and '*Scende la sera*'. '*Scende la sera*', a lament for the carnage of the *Terza Festa*, assumes the same role as *E vo* in *Opera*, and points to the same image of blood in the streets as do the Neruda sections from *Coro*, but in its directness and simplicity outstrips both.

Part I of *La vera storia* interleaves stories told in the opera house and on the street with the bitterly familiar story of revolt and its suppression. Part II takes up that story to the exclusion of all others. Berio directs that the proscenium arch should be completely closed by the façade of a building, into some of whose rooms we can see when lights are lit, and which functions sometimes as a dwelling, sometimes as a barracks or prison. The confined space of the proscenium itself is therefore the street, with street lamps to emphasize the passage of night and day. Those who hurry along it are an anonymous city crowd, and although we hear snatches of texts that in Part I belonged to specific 'characters', they are spoken or sung by unnamed 'passers-by'. The chorus, a massive presence in Part I, are now reduced to a fearful silence broken only by scattered interjections, while disembodied voices sing from the orchestra pit. Everyone moves in fear of a diffused and tentacular oppression, an omnipresent violence. It is one of Berio's most chilling conceptions.

The scenario of Part II is a latter-day, urban version of the scenario familiar to us fron Part I. The first Passer-by is seized by the police, interrogated, and pushed from an upper window to his death. (This image confronted the Milanese audience at the La Scala première with all too specific a memory: on the night of 15 December 1969 the anarchist Giuseppe Pinelli supposedly 'jumped' from the fourth floor of the Police Headquarters in Via

Fatebenefratelli, and fell to his death. This was but one link in a murky chain of events, including bomb outrages and a number of other deaths, that the authorities persisted in viewing as products of left-wing terrorism. Many of them remain unexplained.) A child is again stolen and presumably killed. The authorities institute systematic repression. Guerrilla warfare breaks out in the street, but is contained by the appropriate measures. In the midst of this are two embracing figures: they turn out to be Leonora and Ada, and as 'the people' are reduced to utter submission by the forces of law and order, these characters from a putative opera are joined by others from Part I to give voice to what the chorus can no longer sing: the expression of resignation and tenacious hope that ended the *Quarta Festa*. Finally, Ada is left alone to end Part II as she had ended Part I.

Although the materials of Part II are those of Part I revisited and reworked, this is no simple process. Ex. VII.1 reproduces Berio's own analysis of the relationships between the two parts. From this it is clear that verbally Part II starts in parallel with Part I, but then subjects Calvino's text to a series of excisions and compressions (which nevertheless retain some vestige of the original order), before returning to the original text at the end. By contrast, the musical structure operates an extraordinary series of transpositions and syntheses of material, rather after the manner of the final movement of *Sinfonia*—a parallel that becomes particularly strong when the complex synthesis of Scene VIII resolves into the conclusion of the *Quarta Festa*, and leads into a complete recapitulation of *Il Ricordo*, with which the work ends. But although Part II represents the most complex realization yet of the commentary procedures discussed in Chapter IV, it also draws in new materials. Scene IV puts Berio's talent for pastiche to ironic use as a street reciter (a solitary and songless reminder of the *cantastorie* from Part I) declaims the text of *Il Ratto*, while inside the building the story of the stolen child is re-enacted, and an on-stage accordion player leads the orchestra in a waltz interlarded with a tango. Scene VII contains references of a different sort, for it reworks materials from Berio's own *Sequenza IX* for clarinet to provide a troubled quiescence after the street violence of the previous scene.

In a brief (and reluctant) note to accompany *La vera storia*, which he felt might best be left to narrate and explain itself, Berio commented that 'In Part I, made up of closed numbers, it is the

Ex. VII.1 Outline of structural relations in *La vera storia*

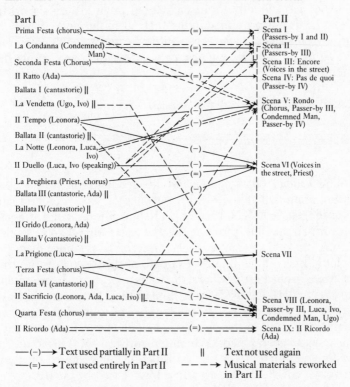

---(−)→ Text used partially in Part II   ‖   Text not used again
---(=)→ Text used entirely in Part II   - - - → Musical materials reworked
                                                    in Part II

action on stage that dominates; in Part II it is musical action . . .
Part I is real and concrete, Part II is oneiric. Part I embraces the
operatic stage, Part II rejects it . . .'. Even within Part I there is a
gradual transfer of energy as a spare, effective theatre music that
allows psychological space for the rich visual input of the stage
spectacle gives way to the intense music of the last eight numbers.
Part II completes the process. It is Berio's richest and most
completely realized example of a 'theatre of the imagination'. The
actions that we see and the words that we hear give theatrical
focus to a drama that is quintessentially musical.

But to draw the listener into the oneiric drama that lies beyond
story-telling can only be done within the framework of an established code. The clear-cut musical and dramatic expositions of
Part I provide that code. And if in Part II materials are folded into
each other to create new musico-dramatic configurations, this is

possible because all the major materials of the opera are related more or less directly to an eight-note pitch group, set out in Ex. VII.2 as it is presented in the first bar of the work. Naturally, the other four notes of the chromatic scale are frequently employed, but either as ancillary pitches, or else to stand over against this pitch nucleus.

Ex. VII.2 Pitch framework for *La vera storia*

The crucial characteristic of this pitch group is the clear differentiation that it provides between an area of chromatic saturation (A to C♯) and an area of highly differentiated intervals —of which the most prominent is the leap from C♯ to E. Such a feature makes for immediately discernible relations between melodic lines. The simplest example of this occurs in the trio, *La Notte*, from Part I, where the affinity between Leonora and Luca is underlined by deriving both of their lines from the basic pitch group, while Ivo's line emphasizes the four missing pitches. (Only at the end of this section, when all three sing together, is this polarity abandoned.) When in turn Luca sings his long aria, *La Prigione*, the core pitches to which his line returns time and again, C, C♯, E, F♯, G, are those highlighted by the basic pitch group (see Ex. VII.5, below).

But any such basic reservoir of pitch resources is of course as much a generator of harmonic characteristics as of melodic ones. And as might be expected, Berio brings these to the fore at the cardinal structural points in *La vera storia*: the four Festas of Part I, the opening of Part II, and the recapitulation of the *Quarta Festa* at the end of Part II. The *Seconda Festa*, for instance, is built from the three chords set out in Ex. VII.3b, to which the stage band adds a B♭ until, overcome by panic, it runs away.

There are strong hints of a partially chromaticized Phrygian mode (transposed up a tone from its usual final on E) in the basic pitch group, and in the *Seconda Festa* Berio makes full use of this F♯-based modal sound. Even in the *Prima Festa*, when the chorus move from speech to song (at F_{10}) with a repertoire of seven chords (Ex. VII.3a) that eventually dissolves into freer writing, this modal element is still present: all chords but two

Ex. VII.3 Harmonic repertoire of the *Prima* and *Seconda Festa* from *La vera storia*

a Prima Festa   *b* Seconda Festa

contain either F♯ A, or F♯ C♯. But the most extensive and important stretch of choral harmony that Berio derives from his basic pitch group is the sequence that closes the *Quarta Festa*, and initiates the recapitulated materials at the end of Part II. The first two sections of this are set out as a harmonic skeleton in Ex. VII.4. The retrograde process that begins within the second section is pursued right back to the opening chord, which then contracts its lowest note, C.

Here we are no longer dealing with modal echoes (though it is perhaps not without significance that F♯ marks the high-point of the sequence). But the continuity with earlier examples of Berio's harmonic thought is striking. Particularly clear is the analogy with

Ex. VII.4 Harmonic summary from the *Quarta Festa* from *La vera storia*

(Anche un giorno)

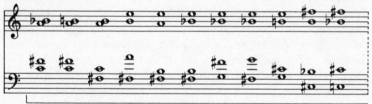

(Ricomincia l'attesa)

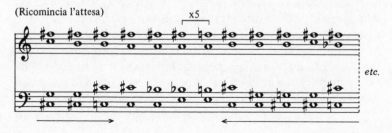

the opening structure of *Sequenza VI* analysed in Chapter IV. Here too the upper line rises to a peak and falls away again in a retrograde. But the essential analogy is in the treatment of voice leading. Lower voices jump to replace each other in the same pitch area—so that each area is characterized by an intermittent chromatic meander. Save where the voices implode upon each other at the end, a gap of at least an augmented fourth is maintained above middle C or C♯, and save for the first three chords, at least an augmented fourth is always maintained between the upper two voices up to that same implosion. There are thus active and empty pitch bands. (The same is true of the chord repertoire used in the *Prima Festa*: see Ex. VII.3a.) And the power of the ear to absorb a fixed pitch class field such as this is fully attested by the aural shock caused when the two chords that should follow on from Ex. VII.4 in the retrograde process are modified so that the top notes are no longer F♯ and E but an alien F, thus marking the start of the descent.

But such block harmony is the exception rather than the rule. *La vera storia*, and even more Berio's next theatrical work, *Un re in ascolto*, depend upon a fundamentally contrapuntal texture in which the ear is led into the exploration of harmonic nuance by the cogency of individual lines. The harmonic palette that he uses by now includes many chords and gestures with strong connotations of other, and more 'functional' vocabularies. But the linear nature of the writing can contain such connotations without disruption. Ex. VII.5, taken from the start of Luca's *La Prigione*, shows a typical example, in which contrapuntal lines (notably those of the horn and cello) are generated by, and split off from, the vocal line. Also typical is Berio's abandonment of the nervous rhythms of his earlier works for a broad, even tactus that will accomodate melodic gestures strongly rooted in the European lyrical tradition.

Part I of *La vera storia* could almost be taken as an encyclopaedia of Berio's melodic techniques. Leonora's aria, *Il Tempo* starts from a highly differentiated fixed field, with typical gaps around which the voice must jump (Ex. VII.6a), and progressively fills them until the full chromatic gamut is available. The duet *Il Grido* for Leonora and Ada is constructed with exemplary parsimony by exploring the possible interactions between two constantly repeated wave-form sequences sharing four common pitches (Ex. VII.6b). And *Il Ricordo*, with which Ada concludes both Parts, is an

Ex. VII.5 *La vera storia, La Prigione,* reduction of D6–11

eloquent example of Berio's rewriting of pre-established melodic lines. It has four sections, the first three providing different settings of the first verse of Calvino's poem, the fourth setting the second verse. But substantial portions of section three reinterpret the line of section one, and the initial sequences of sections two

Ex. VII.6*a* Pitch field from *Il Tempo,* and *b* pitch cycles from
Il Grido from *La vera storia*

a   Il Tempo

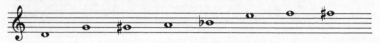

b   Il Grido

(Leonora)   (Ada)

and four are similarly related: thereafter section four must pursue a different melodic course if it is to establish a sense of ending.

Berio's next theatre work, *Un re in ascolto* (literally 'A King Listening') shares with *La vera storia* many of these technical and idiomatic features. But here musical procedures are even more clearly at the heart of the dramatic process, as is appropriate to a work that revolves around the act of listening. One can therefore reverse usual critical procedures, and discuss the musical framework before exploring the verbal and visual images that Berio employs to give concrete focus to it. Like Part I of *La vera storia,* *Un re in ascolto* is written as a series of separate numbers: Arias, Duets, Concertati, and so forth. But on a larger scale they constitute a group of interweaving processes, each clearly marked out from the other. At the still centre of a turning musico-dramatic world are the five arias for Prospero, an old theatrical impresario who is the listener at the heart of the work. All of his arias are constructed from the same fixed field of pitches, set out in Ex. VII.7 and, like Ex. VII.6a, depending upon a clearly differentiated leap with a range of chromatic choice to either side of it, so as to produce a range of intervallic variants within a constantly recurring melodic contour. But if the melodic lines of Prospero's arias are therefore closely related, the orchestral sonorities enveloping those lines are in each case markedly

Ex. VII.7 Prospero's pitch field from *Un re in ascolto*

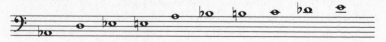

different, and can thus be used to signal the particular dramatic and poetic significance of his penultimate aria, to be discussed below.

Prospero is listening for a woman's voice capable of embodying the female protagonist that he has imagined. During the course of the work, he therefore auditions three singers: each markedly different from the last in vocal character, and in the style of accompaniment that she receives from the on-stage piano, but all united by addressing him with related settings of his own name. Towards the end of the work, the protagonist that he has imagined enters, and develops fragments from *Auditions I* and *II* (and fainter echoes of the relatively recent *Audition III*) into a climactic *tour de force* of melodic invention.

Ex. VII.8 sets side by side a passage from *Audition I* (a), and its elaboration in the Protagonista's *Aria V* (b). The vocal line in Ex. VII.8a is drawn from the static harmonic field with which the stage piano accompanies it. The orchestra either echoes the vocal line, or colours the accompaniment with pianissimo oscillations and trills. Clearly, the Protagonista's melodic line in Ex. VII.8b is a liberal reinterpretation of Ex. VII.8a, but the orchestral accompaniment draws quite different harmonic consequences from it. Below an oscillating G/B♭ that anticipates that of the vocal line, the strings pursue a vigorously mobile harmony characterized (though the reduction cannot show it) by the frequent crossing of lines within upper and lower strings.

The context of Prospero's listening is his theatre, which bustles with activity as his cast rehearse a complex, but as yet only partially coherent spectacle. This generates a third strand: a series of multi-voiced Concertati that accomodate a more diverse range of materials than do the other two. *Concertati I*, *II*, and *IV* involve the chorus, three male singers, Venerdì, a grotesque creature who recites his texts, and an omnipresent and domineering producer (who also has beneath his sway dancers, acrobats, etc.). They are closely connected: all focus upon a more or less explicit G minor, and thus provide a subtle link to Prospero, whose pitch field (see Ex. VII.7) permits passing melodic evocations of the same key. *Concertati I* and *II* make much of another of Berio's pastiche waltzes, which returns as a final echo at the end of *IV*. More strikingly, a section of choral homophony similar in style and function to that from *La vera storia* discussed above, concludes each Concertato. (The analogy is even stronger in

Ex. VII.8*a Un re in ascolto, Audition I*, reduction of bars 38:5−39:2,
plus *b Aria V*, reduction of bars 51:3−52:2

111

Ex. VII.8 (cont.):

(cont.):

Concertato IV, where Berio again uses solo voices that depart, leaving a single singer alone on stage to conclude the work.) *Concertato III* involves different characters, and has a different dramatic function, but maintains a subcutaneous parallel in the persistent use of waltz time, and in organizing a clamour of voices around inner instrumental lines whose linear rise and fall recalls that of the homophonic passages from the other Concertati. Three of the four Concertati are preceded by a Duet.

The pattern created by these interweaving layers is set out in Ex. VII.9. Clearly, there are some simple formal analogies between Parts I and II: the first half of each contains a progression from Duet to Concertato to Audition (preceded in Part II by a purely instrumental *Air*), and the second half of each contains a progression from Prospero singing to Prospero listening, and then via a third item (the ironic *Duet III* between a speaker and a mime in Part I, the conclusive *Concertato IV* in Part II) back to a final Aria from Prospero. This formal skeleton suggests also a dramaturgical progression. The duets, normal vehicles of operatic confrontation, are concentrated in the first part of the work. (*Duet IV* is no more than a brief preface to *Concertato III*.) After the central *Concertato II* of Part I, Prospero's monologues anchor the rest of the structure. And this passing from confrontation to introspection is indeed at the core of the work's dramatic shape. But although the 'story' that gives dramatic focus to this musical structure is as simple, graphic, and universal as any, it offers simply a point of psychological anchorage from which the spectator may make forays into the complexities of Berio's open theatre.

Prospero, intent upon realizing his dreams of 'another theatre', watches the producer rehearse first Venerdì (*Duet I*), then the whole cast (*Concertato I*) with increasing misgiving. After a break in rehearsals to hear the soprano audition, open confrontation erupts (*Duet II*). Is Prospero forever contradicting himself in his attempt to formulate this 'other theatre', or is the producer constantly betraying Prospero's vision by an extravagant assertion of his own creativity? We shall never know. The producer returns to his experiments with renewed determination (*Concertato II*); Prospero retires into his own thoughts about the theatre of the ear (*Aria II*). He hears the mezzo-soprano audition. His 'familiars', Venerdì and the mime, re-enact a parody of his quarrel with the producer (*Duet III*). Left alone (*Aria III*), he sings of a voice

Ex. VII.9 Outline of structural relations in *Un re in ascolto*

Prospero alone	Prospero listens	Producer and Players		
Arias	Auditions	Duets	Concertati	Others

I

I

I

I

II

II

II

(!)

Serenade

III

III

II

III

IV

III

Air

III

IV

V

VI

IV

among the inner voices that says 'die': he tries to tear down some of the producer's scenery, but collapses.

He is found where he fell at the start of Part II by the producer.[5] As those nearest to him realize that he is dying, they react with a hubbub of self-interest (*Concertato III*). His players react with greater integrity, initiating an undisciplined wake. But Prospero has retreated into the world of his 'other' theatre, and himself assumes what was to have been the central role of a listening king, deciphering the ruin of his kingdom, court conspiracy, the infidelity of his wife from what he hears around him. A coloratura soprano comes in to be auditioned, and is compelled to take on the role of his guilty queen: she is led away. Prospero's meditations on listening reach a focal point: he recognizes that his kingdom is not that of the scenery and the spotlights of his theatre, but 'the sea of music' (*Aria IV*). As if summoned by this realization, the female protagonist for whom he had been searching now materializes. She sings (*Aria V*), as had the three vocalists whose auditions she summates, of the irreparable distance between herself and Prospero. His players bid him farewell (*Concertato IV*), and left alone on the stage of his theatre, he dies.

The simplicity of this basic conception belies the complexity by which it was achieved. The initial impetus for *Un re in ascolto* came from Calvino while he was working with Berio on *La vera storia*. He had become engrossed in an essay on 'Listening' that Roland Barthes had written for the Encyclopedia Einaudi,[6] and proposed the topic to Berio as the focus for a theatrical piece. Indeed, he produced a three-act libretto wittily ironizing operatic convention, and revolving around the story of the listening king which emerges first in *Duet III* of *Un re in ascolto*, and then is partially acted out by Prospero in Part II. But as has already been noted, Berio never puts himself in a position where literary structure determines musical structure, and had already played out his interest in operatic convention in *La vera storia*. He therefore threw into the ring the conception of the old theatrical impresario whose 'kingdom' slips from his control. After many exchanges of letters and ideas, Berio was left with the five monologues on listening that form the core of *Un re in ascolto*, and Calvino's letters summarizing their differences in vision in the form of a dialogue between 'I' and 'You', which provided the inspiration for *Duets II* and *III*. Berio now looked about him for complementary materials out of which to build up the work's verbal resources.[7]

The image of *The Tempest*, and of Prospero as the master of a theatre of spirits was already in Berio's mind when, by happy coincidence, Talia Pecker Berio came across a singspiel libretto of 1791, *Die Geisterinsel* by Friedrich Einsiedel and Friedrich Gotter, which was based on *The Tempest*. This Berio used to provide much of the text for the materials upon which director, singers, and chorus are working, and some of the latter part of Venerdi's much-rehearsed recitation. But *The Tempest* also stirred other memories. As was noted in Chapter II, among Berio's literary enthusiasms of the fifties had been W. H. Auden, whose work had provided the starting-point for *Nones*. He now returned to Auden's poem-sequence, *The Sea and the Mirror* (1944), which sought to explore the ambivalent situation in which Shakespeare left his characters at the conclusion of *The Tempest*, where 'both the repentance of the guilty and the pardon of the injured seem more formal than real'.[8] From the Stage-Manager's Prologue to *The Sea and Mirror* Berio took the images of Venerdi's recitation— the carelessly waltzing couple echoed by Berio's own waltz in *Concertati I* and *II*. But it was Auden's fascination with Antonio, Prospero's brother, whose repentance even in Shakespeare's *The Tempest* is patently only skin-deep, that furnished Berio with his most significant material. Auden's poem-sequence gives most of Shakespeare's other characters a chance to draw their own conclusions, but after each Antonio chimes in with a refrain, varied each time, but always reminding Prospero that he cannot reconcile and unify his world, that Antonio remains implacably and immutably 'other'. Berio borrowed these refrains, and combined them with part of Gonzalo's meditation upon the evening sea as he sails home, to produce the texts of the Auditions and the female protagonist's Aria. More all-pervasive, though not specifically quoted, was Auden's long poetic monologue on the all-inclusiveness of Shakespeare, and the transactions that take place between players and audience, *Caliban to the Audience*: both themes that find strong resonances in Berio's own work.

Thus although echoes of *The Tempest* abound throughout *Un re in ascolto*, the play is only present at several removes. A Prospero of sorts there is, and one whose theatre is itself an island. From off-stage we hear sirens, and at one point gun-fire: it would seem that outside the cold anarchy of Part II of *La vera storia* continues unabated. Messages are constantly delivered to Prospero from the world beyond his theatre/island. He ignores them. And when everyone else leaves the island at the end, this Prospero stays on alone, to die. The grotesque, ironic figure of Venerdi owes much to Caliban (though his name, literally 'Friday', has other insular connotations), but remains faithful to Prospero throughout. And Prospero's other attendant, the Mime, is addressed by him as 'Ariel'—yet here is an Ariel who cannot sing. An even stranger reversal attends upon the protagonist. When finally she arrives on stage, she is dressed in the rags of a 'survivor': apparently it is she who has suffered shipwreck, not Ferdinand or the Neapolitan court.

Confronted with such a labyrinth of sources, the temptation to play a sort of scholarly hide-and-seek is considerable. But it is potentially a false trail. In some works, notably *Sinfonia* and *Opera*, Berio does indeed create complex interactions between multiple sources. Here, however, he takes as much as he needs from his various sources to give focus and edge to his 'musical action', and no more. More instructive are the relationships between *Un re in ascolto* and Berio's other theatrical works. Many of the features that make *Opera* both fascinating and problematic here find a more mature and accessible solution. Both works have death as a central theme (it is a constant touchstone in Berio's work, hidden in *Nones*, drowned out in the Simon setting from *Epifanie*, omnipresent in *Sinfonia*, and an essential source of perspective in all the major works that follow). Both play with one of the oldest of theatrical games: the theatre within a theatre, and the drama of rehearsal and performance. Both have interweaving layers of musico-dramatic material, and texts from multiple sources. But where *Opera* demands of the spectator that he operate as an entirely free agent within this open theatre, making his own connections as he goes, *Un re in ascolto* offers a central focus, a protagonist to whom everything can be related as part either of his outer or his inner world. To an audience ready to absorb through empathy, but hesitant when invited to explore a maze of someone else's devising, this is a thread which may lead where otherwise they might never choose to go.

Berio is thus free to pursue his Utopia of an all-embracing, humanistic theatre guided by musical process (a Utopia in which there are strong echoes of Mahler's vision of the symphony, and one whose arduous attainment might tell us a little about why Mahler felt himself in no position to write operas). His own commentary on *Un re in ascolto* took the form of an extension of the dialogues sketched by Calvino in his letters to Berio in order to decipher their differences: now though, Berio assumed the roles of composer, and member of the audience. Above it he placed a quotation from Baudelaire's *Journaux intimes* that explores the singular magic of one of Berio's own most deep-rooted obsessions, a ship in motion. It might serve as epigraph to the aspirations not just of *Un re in ascolto*, but of all of Berio's large-scale works

I believe that the infinite and mysterious charm that is to be found in contemplating a ship, and above all a ship in motion, derives in the first instance from the regularity and symmetry that are one of the primordial needs of the human spirit, just as much as is the complication that follows, and from the generation of all the imaginary curves and figures that the real components of this object execute in space. The poetic idea that detaches itself from this operation of contours in movement is the hypothesis of a vast, immense, complicated, but eurhythmic being, an animal filled with spirit, suffering and giving voice to all the sighs and all the ambitions of humanity.

NOTES

CHAPTER I

1. In his text for Prospero's Aria IV from *Un re in ascolto*.
2. The line can be traced back to Stefano Berio, a late eighteenth-century lawyer who was also an extremely competent 'dilettante' composer. Thereafter the family split: the lawyers and politicians moved to Rome, the musicians stayed in Liguria.
3. Berio, *Two Interviews* (London, 1985), pp. 43–4.
4. In deference to his father's wishes, he also enrolled in the Faculty of Law at Milan University, but abandoned his studies before the first year was out.
5. Berio, *Two Interviews*, pp. 75–6.
6. Other examples will be found in Chapter III, below.

CHAPTER II

1. Phonology examines functional differences between sounds as determinants of meaning in language—whereas phonetics, as Berio was soon to demonstrate, offers the musician a great deal more.
2. Berio's manuscript version of this system is reproduced as Illustration 4 in Berio, *Two Interviews* (Marion Boyars, London, 1985).
3. Similarly, the *Serenata* of 1957 is composed 'against the grain' of a process designed to minimize differentiation: the magic square.
4. Berio, *Two Interviews*, p. 63.
5. It was, ironically, the only major instrumental work of the 1950s about which he published an extensive discussion: see Berio 'Aspetti di artigianato formale', *Incontri musicali: Quaderni internationali di musica contemporanea*, i (Milan, 1956).
6. The score lists ten different sequences, but sequence 5 is simply an erroneous variant of 4.

CHAPTER III

1. See, for instance, Claudio Annibaldi, *The New Grove Dictionary of Music and Musicians* (Macmillan, London, 1980), pp. 554–9. (which should, however, be read with caution, since it contains a number of factual errors).

2. The score is in proportional notation, so that no bar references can be given.

3. But in an instrumental context, he could still engage in agile disguises after the manner of the flute *Sequenza*. For an example from *Sinfonia*, see David Osmond-Smith, *Playing on Words: A Guide to Luciano Berio's* Sinfonia (Royal Musical Association, London, 1985), p. 18.

4. For an extended analysis of *O King*, see ibid., pp. 21–38.

5. Derived from Berio's childhood memories of a turn by Grock, the clown (Adriano Wettach), in which repeated mishaps with his violin produced a plaintive 'Warum?'. 'Why' is echoed time and again by the trombonist manipulating his plunger mute.

6. Chosen because it can be produced by a greater variety of fingerings, each with its own timbre, than any other note on the instrument. Berio demands six different versions. The interplay between them is a cardinal feature of the opening lines.

7. See Berio, 'Du geste et de Piazza Carità', *La Musique et ses problèmes contemporains, Cahiers Renaud-Barrault*, 1 (Paris, 1963).

CHAPTER IV

1. Whose single fleeting appearence as the high Db of Ex. 5.1. is a reference back to the previous section, where it had been missed out of the final ascent.

2. For further examples, see David Osmond-Smith, *Playing on Words: A Guide to Luciano Berio's* Sinfonia (Royal Musical Association, London, 1985), pp. 16, 33, 72, and 81.

3. A detailed account of *Sinfonia* is given ibid.

CHAPTER V

1. Eco's own critical work on Joyce was brought together in an extensive study, *Le poetiche di Joyce*, first published as part of *Opera Aperta* (Bompiani, Milan, 1962), though issued as a separate volume in subsequent editions.

2. For a more detailed description of these and other features of *Thema*, see Berio, 'Poesia e musical—un' esperienza', *Incontri musicali: Quaderni internationali di musica contemporanea*, iii (Milan, 1959).

3. For further details, see International Phonetic Association, *The Principles of the International Phonetic Association*, (IPA, London, 1949).

4. For a more detailed analysis, see David Osmond-Smith, *Playing on*

Words: A Guide to Luciano Berio's Sinfonia (Royal Musical Association, London, 1985), pp. 21–38.

5. For a more detailed examination of the relations between text and music, see Jaques Demierre, "Circles": e. e. cummings lu par Luciano Berio', *Contrechamps*, i, *Luciano Berio* (Lausanne, 1983).

6. He had already operated a similar, though less structured, process of fragmentation upon Lucretius's *De rerum naturae* in *Passaggio:* see Stoianova, *Luciano Berio: Chemins en musique*, La Revue musicale (Paris, 1985), pp. 240–2.

CHAPTER VI

1. For a concise discussion of *Sequenza IX*, see Philippe Albèra, 'Introduction aux neuf Sequenzas', *Contrechamps*, i, *Luciano Berio* (Lausanne, 1983), pp. 91–122.

2. Berio *Two Interviews* (Marion Boyars, London, 1985), p. 148.

3. The relevant poems may all be found, alongside English translations, in Pablo Neruda, *Selected Poems* (Penguin, Harmondsworth, 1975), pp. 38–45, and 102–107.

4. Berio, *Two Interviews* p. 151.

5. Simha Arom 'The Use of Play-back Techniques in the Study of Oral Polyphonies', *Ethomusicology* 20/3 (1976).

6. For a further discussion of *Coro*, see Norbert Dressen, *Sprache und Musik bei Luciano Berio* (Gustar Basse Verlag, Regensburg, 1982), pp. 204–55.

CHAPTER VII

1. Brecht was the focus of much attention amongst Berio's circle at the time. In October 1955, as *Mimusique No. 2/Tre modi per sopportare la vita* was being prepared for performance, Brecht visited Milan to observe preparations for Giorgio Strehler's production of *The Three-penny Opera*. Bruno Maderna was Musical Director of both productions, and Berio was given the chance to meet Brecht, who remained a permanent influence upon his approach to theatre.

2. Once refined, in *Sinfonia*, into a group of eight amplified voices, this disposition became standard in Berio's stage work: such groups sing from the pit in *Opera*, and the second act of *La vera storia*.

3. For an extended analysis of A-Ronne, see Norbert Dressen, *Sprache und Musik bei Luciano Berio* (Gustav Bosse Verlag, Regensburg, 1982) pp. 157–203.

4. A perspective prompted by the work of the literary theorist, Mikhail Bakhtin: see particularly his *Rabelais and His World* (The M.I.T. Press, Cambridge, Massachusetts, 1968) pp. 1–58 and 196–277.
5. Berio had originally conceived the work as running continuously, without an interval.
6. Roland Barthes' 'Ascolto', *Enciclopedia Einaudi* (Einaudi, Turin, 1976).
7. Calvino meanwhile reformulated his original conception as a short story with the same title, published in Italo Calvino, *Sotto il sole giaguaro* (Garzanti, Milan, 1986) pp. 59–92, trans. William Weaver as *Under the Jaguar Sun* (Harcourt Brace Jovanovitch, New York, 1988).
8. Humphrey Carpenter, *W. H. Auden: A Biography* (Allen & Unwin, London, 1981) p. 325.

WORK LIST

Authors of texts and choreographers are given in brackets immediately after the title. Berio's two principal publishers, Suvini Zerboni and Universal Edition, are abbreviated throughout as SZ and UE respectively. Where no other indication is given, clarinets are in Bb, and trumpets are in C.

1937

Pastorale for piano.

1939

Toccata for piano duet.

1944

Preludio a una festa marina for string orchestra.

1946

O bone Jesu for choir.
Divertimento for violin, viola, and cello. RCA Revised 1985.

1946–7

Tre canzoni popolari (Anon.) for voice and piano.

1947

Tre pezzi for three clarinets. 1st perf.: Milan, 1947.
Petite Suite pour piano. UE 1st perf.: Como, 1948.

1946–8

Tre liriche greche for voice and piano (which include 'E di te nel tempo', on occasion listed separately).

1948

Quintetto for wind.
Due canti siciliani for tenor and male chorus.
Ad Hermes for voice and piano. 1st perf.: Oneglia, 1948, Cavour.

1949

Due pezzi sacri for two sopranos, piano, two harps, timpani, and twelve bells.
Magnificat for two sopranos, chorus (SSAATB), and orchestra (flute, oboe, 2 clarinets—2 horns, 2 trumpets, 2 trombones—timpani, percussion, vibraphone, 2 pianos—double-bass). Belwyn-Mills. 1st perf.: Turin, 1971, Berberian, Ross, Juilliard Ensemble, cond. Berio.
Concertino for solo clarinet, solo violin, harp, celesta, and strings. UE 1st perf.: Milan, 1950, Borisov, orchestra of Conservatorio students, cond. Berio. Revised 1951 and 1970.

1950

Tre vocalizzi for voice and piano.

Opus No. Zoo (Cathy Berberian) for reciter, two clarinets, and two horns. 1st perf.: Milan, 1952, Berberian. Incorporates material from unfinished *Quartetto* for wind. Revised 1951 for wind quintet. Revised 1970 with text (Rhoda Levine, based on Berberian) recited by instrumentalists. UE 1st perf.: 1971, New York, Dorian Quintet.

Deus meus for voice and three instruments. 1st perf.: Milan, 1952, Berberian, Rensa, Abbado, Bergonzi.
Sonatina for flute, two clarinets, and bassoon.
Due pezzi for violin and piano. SZ 1st perf.: Tanglewood, 1952, Maazel, Lipkin. Revised 1966 (at which time the original date of composition was erroneously given as 1949).

Study for string quartet. 1st perf.: Tanglewood, 1952, quartet of students. RCA Revised 1985.
El mar la mar (Rafael Alberti) for two sopranos, flute, clarinet, guitar, accordion, and double-bass. Reduction for two sopranos and piano, 1953. Arranged for soprano, mezzo-soprano, flute (piccolo), two clarinets (second plus bass clarinet), harp, accordion, cello, double-bass, 1969. UE 1st perf.: Royan, 1969, Berberian, Rist, Juilliard Ensemble cond. Berio.
Quattro canzoni popolari for voice and piano. The *Tre canzoni popolari* of 1946–7 plus a fourth setting, 'Avendo gran disio' (Jacopo da Lentini). UE 1st perf.: Milan, 1952, Berberian, Berio. Revised 1973.

Cinque variazioni for piano. SZ 1st perf.: Milan, 1953, Berio. Revised 1966.

Mimusique No. 2 orchestra (piccolo, two flutes, two oboes, three Bb clarinets (plus Eb and bass), two bassoons, double bassoon —four horns, four trumpets, three trombones—timpani, cymbals, tam-tam, triangle, gong, side-drum, vibraphone, glockenspiel, harp, celesta). SZ Incorporated into *Mimusique No. 2/Tre modi per sopportase la vita* (1955).

1953

Mimusique No. 1 for single-track tape.
Chamber Music (Joyce) for female voice, cello, clarinet, and harp. SZ 1st perf.: Milan, 1953, Berberian.

1953-4

Variazioni for chamber orchestra (piccolo, flute, oboe, 2 clarinets, 2 bassoons—2 horns, 2 trumpets, 1 trombone—strings (8.8.6.4.3) SZ 1st perf.: NDR Hamburg, 1955, cond. Sanzogno.

1954

Nones for orchestra (piccolo, 2 flutes, 2 oboes, 2 clarinets, 2 bassoons, double bassoon—4 horns, 2 trumpets, 3 trombones, tuba—timpani, bass drum, triangle, 2 suspended cymbals, 2 side-drums, 2 tam-tams, celesta, glockenspiel, vibraphone, xylophone—electric guitar, harp, piano—violins A-B-C (10.10.10), violas (10), cellos (8), double-basses (9). SZ 1st perf.: RAI, Turin, 1955, cond. Maderna.
Ritratto di città (Roberto Leydi) for single-track tape. Composed with Bruno Maderna. 1st perf.: RAI, 1955.

1952-5

Mimusique No.2/Tre modi per sopportare la vita (scenario: Roberto Leydi) for mimes and orchestra (as in *Mimusique No. 2*. Includes a new 'Rhumba-Ramble'. SZ 1st perf.: Bergamo, 1955, cond. Maderna.

1955

Mutazioni for one-track tape. 1st perf.: RAI Milan, 1956.

1955–6

Quartetto for strings. SZ 1st perf.: Vienna, 1959, Die Reihe Quartet.

Allelujah I for six instrumental groups (I: 4 flutes (plus 3 piccolos), 2 oboes, 2 clarinets, bass clarinet, 8 cellos; II: Eb clarinet, alto saxophone, tenor saxophone, 2 bassoons, double bassoon, 6 double-basses; III: celesta, vibraphone, marimbaphone, xylophone, 2 harps, piano, glockenspiel; IV: 4 horns, 5 trumpets, percussion (2 side-drums, 3 tom-toms, bass drum, 2 suspended cymbals, gong, triangle), bells; V: 4 horns, 3 trombones, tuba, timpani; VI: 10 violins, 10 violas). SZ 1st perf.: WDR Cologne, 1957, cond. Gielen. Withdrawn and substantially reworked to form *Allelujah II* (1957–8).

Produced in collaboration with Maderna a number of electronic studies. There are records of the following: *Musica di scena No. 9, Studio No. 3, Studio No. 4,* plus *Film Music* by Berio alone. For all of these, 1st perf.: RAI Milan, 1956.

1956

Variazioni 'ein Mädchen oder Weibchen' for two basset horns and strings. Schott/UE 1st perf.: Donaueschingen, 1956, Lemser, Meier, Südwestfunkorchester, cond. Rosbaud.

1957

Perspectives for two-track tape. SZ 1st perf.: Milan, 1957.

Divertimento for orchestra (3 flutes (plus 2 piccolos), 2 oboes, cor anglais, Eb clarinet, 2 Bb clarinets, bass clarinet, 5 saxophonists (variously playing 1 soprano, two altos, 1 tenor, 1 baritone, or 1 alto, 2 tenors, 2 baritones, or 2 altos, 2 tenors, 1 baritone, or 2 Bb clarinets, 2 tenors, 1 baritone), 2 bassoons, double bassoon—2

horns, 5 C trumpets (plus 1 F trumpet), 3 trombones, tuba—
timpani, 3 bongos, claves, 3 tom-toms, 3 suspended cymbals,
3 tam-tams, 5 cencerros, triangle, 2 side-drums, 3 temple-
blocks—electric guitar, vibraphone, marimbaphone, xylophone,
celesta, glockenspiel, harp, piano—strings). 1st movement, 'Dark
rapture crawl', by Maderna, 2nd and 3rd movements, 'Scat Rag'
and 'Rhumba-Ramble' (the latter from *Mimusique No. 2/Tre modi
per sopportare la vita*) by Berio. SZ 1st perf.: RAI Rome, 1957,
cond. Maderna.
Serenata for flute and fourteen instruments (oboe, cor anglais,
clarinet, bass clarinet, bassoon, horn, trumpet, trombone, harp,
piano, solo strings). SZ 1st perf.: Paris, Gazzelloni, cond. Boulez.

1957–8

Allelujah II for five instrumental groups (I: celesta, vibraphone,
marimbaphone, electric guitar, 2 harps, piano, 11 bells, 2 bongos,
9 chinese gongs, tambourine, triangle, 6 double-basses; II: 4
flutes (plus 2 piccolos and alto flute), 2 clarinets, bass clarinet,
2 alto saxophones, timpani, xylophone, 5 cencerros, triangle,
4 cellos; III: 4 horns, 3 trombones, double-bass tuba, 3 tam-tams,
3 suspended cymbals, 10 violins; IV: 2 oboes, cor anglais, Eb
clarinet, 2 bassoons, double bassoon, 3 trumpets, 2 side-drums,
3 tom-toms, 4 temple-blocks, glockenspiel, 4 cellos; V: 2 tenor
saxophones, 4 horns, 3 trumpets, 2 trombones, tuba, 2 log drums,
10 violas). SZ 1st perf.: RAI Rome, 1958, cond. Maderna and
Berio.

1958

Thema (Omaggio a Joyce) for two-track tape with the recorded
voice of Cathy Berberian. SZ 1st perf.: Naples, 1958.
Sequenza for flute. SZ 1st perf.: Darmstadt, 1958, Gazzelloni.

1952–9

Allez Hop, 'racconto mimico' (scenario: Calvino) for mimes and
orchestra (3 flutes (plus 2 piccolos), 2 oboes, cor anglais, Eb

clarinet, 2 Bb clarinets, bass clarinet, alto, tenor, and baritone saxophones, 2 bassoons, double bassoon—4 horns, 4 trumpets, 3 trombones, tuba—harp, piano, electric guitar—celesta, timpani, 3 tom-toms, 3 suspended cymbals, 3 tam-tams, bells, xylophone, wood-blocks, tambourine, claves, 3 temple-blocks, maracas, 3 bongos, 2 side-drums, marimbaphone, glockenspiel, snare drum, bass drum, cencerros, triangle, vibraphone—strings (12.10.8.6) SZ. Performances have also included two songs, the music for which is not printed in the score. 1st perf.: Venice, 1959, Berberian, cond. Sanzogo. Revised 1968. 1st perf.: Bologna, 1968, Berberian cond. Berio. Incorporates materials from *Mimusique No. 2/Tre modi per sopportare la vita* including 'Rhumba-Ramble', and 'Scat Rag' from *Divertimento*.

<h2 style="text-align:center">1958–9</h2>

Tempi Concertati for solo flute, violin, two pianos, and four instrumental groups disposed as follows: I: violin, oboe, horn, double-bass, piano; II: bass clarinet, trumpet, 2 violas, marimbaphone, vibraphone, harp, triangle, 4 temple-blocks, 2 bongos, 2 congas, 2 side-drums, 2 suspended cymbals, 3 tubular bells; solo flute; III: clarinet, tenor trombone, 2 cellos, xylophone, glockenspiel, harp, 5 cencerros, 4 wood-blocks, 2 bongos, 3 tom-toms, 2 tam-tams, 3 tubular bells; IV: piccolo, cor anglais, clarinet, bassoon, piano, celesta. UE 1st perf.: NDR Hamburg, 1960, Gazzelloni, Schneeberger, A. and A. Kontarsky, cond. Bour.

<h2 style="text-align:center">1959</h2>

Différences for flute, clarinet, harp, viola, cello, and tape. UE 1st perf.: Paris, 1959, cond. Boulez.
Quaderni I for orchestra (4 flutes (plus 2 piccolos), 3 oboes, cor anglais, 3 Bb clarinets (plus 1 Eb clarinet), 3 bassoons, double bassoon—6 horns, 4 trumpets, 3 trombones (plus 1 tenor-bass), bass trombone, tenor tuba (plus bass tuba)—glockenspiel, celesta, 2 harps, vibraphone, xylophone, marimbaphone, 3 percussionists: I: 2 spring coils, 2 tam-tams, tom-tom, 5 temple-blocks, 3 wood-blocks, side-drum, 2 bongos, timpani, 3 cowbells, bells; II: 2

spring coils, tam-tam, 3 tom-toms, high kettledrum, 3 wood-blocks, side-drum, claves, guiro, grelôts, 5 cencerros, 3 suspended cymbals, 2 bongos, 3 cowbells, snare drum; III: 2 spring coils, tam-tam, bass drum, snare drum, whip, side drum, tambourine, 2 congas, 3 cowbells, 3 chinese gongs—violins A-B-C (8.8.8), violas (8), cellos (8), double basses (6)). UE 1st perf.: Cologne, 1960, SüdwestfunksOrchester cond. Rosbaud. (= *Epifanie A,B,* and *C*)

1960

Momenti for four-track tape. UE 1st perf.: NDR Hamburg, 1960.
Circles (cummings) for female voice, harp, and two percussionists. UE 1st perf.: Tanglewood, 1960, Berberian, members of the Boston Symphony Orchestra, cond. Burgin.

1960–1

Visage for two-track tape, with the recorded voice of Cathy Berberian. UE 1st perf.: RAI Milan, 1961.

1961

Quaderni II for orchestra (as in *Quaderni I*). UE 1st perf.: Vienna, 1961, SüdwestfunksOrchester cond. Rosbaud. (= *Epifanie D,E,* and *F*).

1959–62

Epifanie (Proust, Joyce, Machado, Simon, Brecht, Sanguineti) for female voice and orchestra (as in *Quaderni I*). UE 1st perf (minus *Epifanie G*): Donaueschingen, 1961, Berberian, Südwestfunks-Orchester cond. Rosbaud. Incorporates *Quaderni I–III*. Revised 1965.

Quaderni III for orchestra (as in *Quaderni I*). UE 1st perf.:
Los Angeles, 1963, Los Angeles Philharmonic, cond. Mehta.
(= *Epifanie G, D,* and *C*).

Passaggio (Edoardo Sanguineti) '*messa in scena*' for soprano, Chorus
A (in the pit), Chorus B (of five groups of speakers in the
auditorium), and orchestra (2 flutes (plus 2 piccolos), E♭ clarinet,
B♭ clarinet, bass clarinet, alto saxophone, tenor saxophone,
bassoon, double bassoon—horn, 2 trumpets, 2 tenor trombones,
tuba—harmonium, electric guitar, harp—viola, cello, double-
bass—5 percussionists: I: marimbaphone, snare drum, wood-
chimes, high-hat, slide whistle, rattle, guiro, maracas; II: 2
bongos, 3 tom-toms, 5 wood-blocks, quichas, bells, 2 cymbals,
glass chimes, 2 gongs, 2 triangles, 2 spring coils, slide whistle,
sleigh-bells, log drum, wood chimes; III: vibraphone, snare
drum, 2 bongos, 2 tumbas, tambourine, bass drum, 2 tam-tams,
5 cowbells, 5 temple-blocks, sand-block, 2 spring coils, slide
whistle, log drum; IV: glockenspiel, 2 bongos, 5 cencerros, 2 tam-
tams, quichas, 2 cymbals, glass chimes, whip, 2 spring coils, slide
whistle, log drum; V: xylophone, snare drum, high-hat, wood-
chimes, guiro, maracas, slide whistle, rattle). UE 1st perf.: Milan,
1963, Tavolaccini, Coro della Scala, Kammersprechchor Zürich,
cond. Berio.

Esposizione (Edoardo Sanguineti, chor. Ann Halprin) for mezzo-
soprano, 2 childrens' voices, dancers, 14 instruments, and four-
track tape (precise details of instrumentation are no longer
available, but the ensemble corresponded roughly to that of
Laborintus II). 1st perf.: Venice, 1963, Berberian, Dancers' Workshop of San Francisco, cond. Berio. Withdrawn and reworked to
form part of *Laborintus II*.

Sequenza II for harp. UE 1st perf.: Darmstadt, 1963, Pierre.

Sincronie for string quartet. UE 1st perf.: Grinnell, Iowa, Lenox Quartet, 1964.

1964

Traces (Susan Oyama) for soprano, mezzo-soprano, two actors, two choruses, and orchestra (2 flutes, 3 clarinets, 3 saxophones, bassoon—horn, 3 trumpets, 3 trombones, tuba—harp—3 percussionists—viola, cello, double-bass). UE 1st perf.: uncertain, but 1964/5 cond. Berio, followed by Buffalo, 1965, cond. Foss. Withdrawn after 1968. Some of its materials were reworked in *Opera* (1969–70).
Folk Songs for mezzo-soprano and seven instruments (flute, clarinet, 2 percussionists, harp, viola, cello). UE 1st perf.: Oakland, California, 1964, Berberian cond. Berio. Incorporates 'Ballo' and 'La donna ideale' from *Tre canzoni popolari* (1946–47). Arranged for mezzo-soprano and orchestra (2 flutes, oboe, 2 clarinets, bassoon—horn, trumpet, trombone—2 percussionists—harp—strings). UE 1st perf.: Zurich, 1973, Berberian, Zürich Kammerorchester cond. Berio.
Chemins I on *Sequenza II* for harp and orchestra (3 flutes, 3 oboes, 3 Bb clarinets (plus 1 bass clarinet), 2 bassoons, double bassoon—4 horns, 4 C trumpets, 3 tenor trombones, bass tuba—2 harps, piano, celesta, harpsichord—violins A-B-C (8.8.8), violas (8), cellos (8), double-basses (8)). UE 1st perf.: Donaueschingen, 1965, Pierre, SüdwestfunksOrchester cond. Bour.
Rounds for harpsichord. UE 1st perf.: Basle, 1965, Vischer. Transcribed for piano, 1967. UE 1st perf.: 1968, New York, Spiegelmann.

1965

Wasserklavier for piano. UE 1st perf.: Brescia, 1970, Ballista.
Laborintus II (Sanguineti) for three female voices, eight actors, speaker, instruments (flute, 3 clarinets (plus 1 bass clarinet)—3 trumpets, 3 trombones—2 harps—2 percussionists: I: 'traps',

vibraphone, wood-blocks, guiro, 2 tam-tams, spring coils, grelôts; II: 'traps', wood-blocks, guiro, spring coils, maracas, claves, grelôts, tam-tam—2 cellos, double-bass), and tape. UE 1st perf.: Paris, 1965, cond. Berio.

1965–6

Sequenza III for voice. UE 1st perf.: Radio Bremen, 1966, Berberian.
Sequenza IV for piano. UE 1st perf.: St Louis, 1966, de Carvalho.

1966

Gesti for recorder. UE 1st perf.: 1966, Brüggen.
Sequenza V for trombone. UE 1st perf.: San Francisco, 1966, Dempster.

1967

Sequenza VI for viola. UE 1st perf.: New York, 1967, Trampler. Transcribed for cello 1981 by Rohan de Saram. UE 1st perf.: London, 1981, de Saram.
Chemins II on *Sequenza VI* for viola and nine instrumentalists (flute, clarinet, trombone, electric organ, harp, marimbaphone (plus tam-tam), vibraphone, viola, cello). UE 1st perf.: Copenhagen, 1968, Trampler.
O King for mezzosoprano and five instruments (flute, clarinet, piano, violin, cello). UE 1st perf.: Baldwin-Wallace College, Berea, Ohio, 1967, Aeolian Players.

1968

Chemins III on *Chemins II* for viola, nine instruments (as in *Chemins II*, but with vibraphone and marimbaphone players also playing a tam-tam and a side-drum) and orchestra (piccolo, 3 flutes, 3 clarinets, bass clarinet, 2 bassoons, double bassoon—4 horns, 4 trumpets, 3 trombones, tuba—harp, celesta—strings).

133

UE 1st perf.: Paris, 1968, Trampler, Ensemble Musique Vivante cond. Berio. Revised 1973 for viola and orchestra (as in the previous version, but with the addition of 3 saxophones).

1968–9

Sinfonia (Lévi-Strauss, Beckett, Berio) for eight voices and orchestra (piccolo, 3 flutes, E♭ clarinet, 3 B♭ clarinets, 2 oboes, cor anglais, alto saxophone, tenor saxophone, 2 bassoons, double bassoon—4 horns, 4 trumpets, 3 trombones, bass tuba—harp, piano, electric organ, electric harpsichord—3 percussionists: I: timpani, glockenspiel, tam-tam, snare drum, bongos, guiro; II: marimbaphone, tam-tam, cymbal, bass drum, snare drum, bongos, tambourine, 3 wood-blocks, whip, guiro, sleigh-bells, triangle; III: vibraphone, tam-tam, cymbal, bass drum, snare drum, bongos, tambourine, castanets, guiro, sleigh-bells, 2 triangles—violins A-B-C (8.8.8), violas (8), cellos (8), double-basses (8)). UE 1st perf.: New York, 1968, Swingle Singers, NY Phil. cond. Berio (first four movements only). Incorporates *O King* (1967). 1st perf. of complete work: 1969, Donaueschingen, Swingle Singers, SüdwestfunksOrchester, cond. Bour.
Questo vuol dire che for three female voices, small choir, tape, and other available resources. UE 1st perf.: (incomplete) as *Cela veut dire que* Royan, 1969, Maderna, Berberian, Mantovani, Legrand, Swingle Singers. 1st complete perf.: Rome, 1970, Eco, Berberian, Mantovani, Legrand, Swingle Singers, cond. Berio.

1969

Sequenza VII for oboe and sound source. UE 1st perf.: Basle, 1969, Holliger.
Erdenklavier for piano. UE 1st perf.: Bergamo, 1970, Ballista.
Air (Striggio), from *Opera*, for soprano and orchestra (2 flutes, oboe, 2 clarinets, alto saxophone, tenor saxophone, bassoon, double bassoon—3 horns—vibraphone (plus tam-tam), marimbaphone (plus tam-tam), 3 tam-tams and triangle—electric organ, 2 pianos—violas, cellos, double basses). UE 1st perf.: Rovereto, 1971, Salvetta. Arranged 1970 for soprano, violin, viola, cello, and piano.

Opera (Berio, Furio Colombo, Umberto Eco, Alessandro Striggio, Susan Yankowitz with the Open Theatre of New York) for ten actors, 2 sopranos, tenor, baritone, vocal ensemble (SSAATTBB), orchestra (2 flutes (plus 1 piccolo), oboe, 2 clarinets, alto and tenor saxophone, bassoon, double bassoon—3 horns, 3 trumpets, 2 trombones, tuba—percussion, piano, electric organ, electric guitar—violin, 6 violas, 4 cellos, 4 double-basses), and tape. UE 1st perf.: Santa Fe, 1970, Tracy, Shuttleworth, Perry, Lombardi, Open Theatre Ensemble, cond. Davies.

Revised 1977 to include *Agnus* (1971) and *E vo'* (1972). For this version, orchestra of 2 flutes, 2 oboes, 3 clarinets, alto and tenor saxophone, bassoon, double bassoon—3 horns, 3 trumpets, 3 trombones, tuba—4 percussionists, marimbaphone plus xylophone, 2 pianos, electronic organ, electric guitar—strings. For the 1979 production soloists were soprano, mezzo-soprano, alto, tenor, baritone. Two other movements from *Opera* may also be performed separately: *Air* (1969), and *Melodrama* (1970).

1970

Melodrama (Berio), from *Opera*, for tenor and instruments (flute, clarinet—3 tam-tams, rattle, claves, 2 bongos, sleigh-bells, vibraphone—electric organ—violin, cello, double-bass). UE 1st perf.: Sienna, 1971, Handt, London Sinfonietta, cond. Berio.

Chemins IIb, reworking of *Chemins II* for large ensemble (2 flutes (plus 1 piccolo), oboe, 2 clarinets, alto and tenor saxophone, bassoon, double bassoon—2 horns, 3 C trumpets, 2 trombones, tuba—vibraphone (plus snare drum and tam-tam), marimbaphone (plus tam-tam), tam-tam (plus snare drum and bass drum)—electric guitar, electronic organ, piano—solo violin, 6 violas, 4 cellos, 3 double basses). UE 1st perf.: Berlin, 1970, cond. Masson.

Memory for electronic piano and harpsichord. UE 1st perf.: New York, 1972, Serkin, Berio. Revised 1973.

Ora (Berio, Essam, after Virgil) for soprano, mezzo-soprano, flute, cor anglais, small choir, ensemble (3 oboes, 2 clarinets, bass clarinet, 2 saxophones, 2 bassoons—2 cellos) and orchestra (2 flutes—2 horns, 2 trombones—8 + 8 + 8 violins, 8 violas, 6 cellos, 6 double basses) to be divided into two roughly equal ensembles. 1st perf.: Detroit, 1971, Swingle Singers, Detroit Symphony Orchestra, cond. Berio. Withdrawn after 1975.

Bewegung for orchestra (3 flutes, 2 oboes, cor anglais, 2 clarinets, bass clarinet, alto and tenor saxophone, 2 bassoons, double bassoon—4 horns, 4 trumpets, 3 trombones, tuba—vibraphone, marimbaphone, 5 tam-tams—piano, electronic organ, harp—strings). UE 1st perf.: Glasgow, 1971, Scottish National Orch. cond. Berio. Revised 1984.

Bewegung II, as *Bewegung* plus baritone line (Virgil) added in 1972, 1st perf.: Rotterdam, 1972, Desderi, Rotterdam Philharmonic Orchestra cond. Berio. Subsequently withdrawn.

Agnus for two sopranos, three clarinets, electronic organ (or other sound source). UE 1st perf.: Ball State University, Muncie, Indiana, 1971, Scheurer, Sambuco.

Chemins IIc: Chemins IIb plus bass clarinet. UE 1st perf.: Rotterdam, 1972, Sparnaay, cond. Berio.

E vo' for soprano and instruments (flute, oboe, 3 clarinets—trumpet, trombone—3 cowbells—electronic organ, piano—violin, viola, cello, double-bass). UE 1st perf.: Rovereto, 1972, Salvetta.

Après Visage (chor. Rudi van Dantzig) for tape and orchestra. 1st perf.: Hague, 1972, Nationale Ballet, Residentie Orkest, cond. Tabachnik. Withdrawn.

Recital I (for Cathy) (Berio, based on Moretti and Sanguineti) for mezzo-soprano and seventeen instruments (2 oboes, 2 clarinets —2 horns, trumpet, trombone—percussion—harp, 3 pianos—solo strings). UE 1st perf.: Lisbon, 1972, Berberian, London Sinfonietta cond. Berio. Incorporates *Memory*.

Concèrto for two pianos and orchestra (piccolo, 2 flutes, 2 oboes, cor anglais, E♭ clarinet, 2 B♭ clarinets, bass clarinet, alto and tenor saxophones, 3 bassoons, double bassoon—3 horns, 3 trumpets, 3 trombones, bass tuba—electronic organ, piano, marimba, 6 tom-toms/bongos, 6 cowbells—strings). UE 1st perf.: New York, 1973, Canino, Ballista, New York Philharmonic cond. Boulez.

1973

Still for orchestra (3 flutes, 2 oboes, cor anglais, 3 clarinets, bass clarinet, alto and tenor saxophone, 2 bassoons, double bassoon —4 horns, 4 trumpets, 3 trombones, bass tuba—vibraphone, marimbaphone, 4 bongos, 2 tom-toms, 3 tam-tams—piano, electronic organ, harp—strings). UE 1st perf.: Glasgow, 1973, Scottish National Orch. cond. Gibson. Withdrawn.
Linea (chor. Felix Blaska) for two pianos, marimbaphone, and vibraphone. UE 1st perf.: Grenoble, 1974, Ballets Felix Blaska, K. and M. Labeque, Drouet, Gualda.

1973-4

Cries of London for six voices. 1st perf.: Edinburgh, 1975, King's Singers. Revised and extended 1975 for eight voices. UE 1st perf.: La Rochelle, 1977, Swingle II.
Eindrücke for orchestra (as for *Still* (1973)) UE 1st perf.: Zurich, 1974, Tonhalle-Orchester, cond. Leinsdorf.

1974

Calmo (in memoriam Bruno Maderna) (Homer) for soprano and instruments (flute, oboe, 2 clarinets, bassoon—horn, 2 trumpets, trombone—solo strings). UE 1st perf.: Milan, 1974, Paoletti, cond. Berio. Recomposed 1988-9.
Points on the Curve to Find . . . for piano and twenty-three

instruments (3 flutes, oboe, cor anglais, 3 clarinets, alto (plus tenor) saxophone, 2 bassoons—2 horns, 2 trumpets, trombone, bass tuba—celesta—viola, 2 cellos, double-bass). UE 1st perf.: Donaueschingen, 1974, de Bonaventura, cond. Bour.

Per la dolce memoria di quel giorno, ballet based on Petrarch's *I trionfi* (chor. Maurice Béjart) for voices (Marzocchi, Yeffet, Saito), piano (Berio), and orchestra (Orchestre du Théâtre de la Monnaie cond. Berio) on tape. UE 1st perf.: Florence, 1974.

1974–5

A-Ronne, radiophonic documentary for five actors on a poem by Sanguineti. UE 1st perf.: KRO Radio, Hilversum, 1974. Concert version for eight voices, 1975. UE 1st perf.: Liège, 1975, Swingle II.

Chants parallèles for tape. UE 1st perf.: ORTF Paris, 1975.

1975

Chemins IV on *Sequenza VII* for oboe and strings (3 violins 3 violas 3 'cellos 2 double-basses). UE 1st perf.: London, 1975, Holliger, London Sinfonietta, cond. Berio.

Diario immaginario (Sermonti, after Molière's Le malade imaginaire), radio piece for voices (Bonacelli, Berberian, Mazzochi, Ingrati, Petracchi), chorus, and orchestra (Coro Maschile e Orchestra Sinfonica di Roma della RAI cond. Pressburger) on tape. UE 1st perf.: RAI Florence, 1975.

Fa-Si for organ with registration assistants. UE 1st perf.: Rovereto, 1975.

Quattro versioni originali della Ritirata notturna di Madrid di L. Boccherini sovrapposte e trascritte per orchestra (3 flutes (plus piccolo), 2 oboes, cor anglais, 3 clarinets, 2 bassoons, double bassoon—4 horns, 4 trumpets, 3 trombones, tuba—timpani, 2 snare drums, bass drum, triangle—harp—strings). UE 1st perf.: Milan, 1975, cond. Bellugi.

1975-6

Coro (Folk texts, Neruda) for forty voices (10 S. 10 A. 10 T. 10 B.) and instruments (4 flutes (plus 2 piccolos), oboe, cor anglais, E♭ clarinet, B♭ clarinet, bass clarinet, alto and tenor saxophone, 2 bassoons, double bassoon—3 horns, 4 trumpets, 3 trombones, tenor and bass tuba—electronic organ, piano, 2 percussionists: I: 5 cowbells, 3 tom-toms, 5 tam-tams, snare drum, chimes, nakers, guiro, sleigh-bells, maracas, crotales, rattle, castanets; II: 3 wood-blocks, 2 bongos, 3 tom-toms, 5 tam-tams, bass drum, tambourine, small bells, guiro, sleigh-bells, crotales—3 violins, 4 violas, 4 cellos, 3 double basses). UE 1st perf.: Donaueschingen, 1976, WDR Orch. cond. Berio. Extended 1977. 1st perf. of complete version: London, 1977, same forces.

1976-7

Sequenza VIII for violin. UE 1st perf.: La Rochelle, 1977, Chiarappa. *Ritorno degli snovidenia* for cello and small orchestra (3 flutes, 2 oboes, 2 clarinets, bass clarinet, alto saxophone, 2 bassoons— 2 horns, 2 trumpets, 2 trombones, bass tuba—piano—3 violins, 3 violas, 3 cellos, 2 double basses). UE 1st perf.: Basle, 1977, Rostropovich, cond. Sacher.

1978

Les mots sont allés for cello. UE 1st perf.: Basle, 1978, Rostropovich. *Encore* for orchestra (2 piccolos, 2 flutes, 2 oboes, cor anglais, E♭ clarinet, B♭ clarinet, bass clarinet, saxophone, 2 bassoons, double bassoon—3 horns, 3 trumpets, 3 trombones, tuba—timps, percussion—harp, celesta, piano—strings). UE 1st perf.: Rotterdam, 1978, cond. Zinman. The basis for Part II, Scene III of *La vera storia*.

1980

Chemins V for clarinet and digital system. UE 1st perf.: Paris, 1980, Arrignon. Withdrawn.

Sequenza IX for clarinet, drawn from *Chemins V*. UE 1st perf.: 1980, Arrignon. Transcribed for saxophone as *Sequenza IXb*, 1981. UE 1st perf.: London, 1981, Harle. Materials from the *Sequenza* reworked in Part II, Scene VII of *La vera storia*.

1977–81

La vera storia (Calvino), opera in two parts for two sopranos, mezzo-soprano, two tenors, baritone, bass, at least two *cantastorie* (ballad singers), vocal ensemble (SSAATTBB), chorus, three speakers, mimes, dancers, acrobats, orchestra (4 flutes (plus 2 piccolos), oboe, cor anglais, E♭ clarinet, 2 B♭ clarinets, bass clarinet, alto and tenor saxophones, 2 bassoons, double bassoon —3 horns, 3 trumpets, 3 trombones, tuba—timpani, 2 percussionists—harp, 2 pianos, electronic organ—strings), stage band (piccolo, 2 flutes, 3 clarinets, alto and tenor saxophone— 3 horns, 3 trumpets, 2 flugelhorns, 2 trombones, tuba—percussion). Also on stage: 2 guitars, accordion, violin, piccolo, pianola, wind machine, hooters, sirens, whistles. UE 1st perf.: Milan, 1982, di Credico, Luccardi, Lumini, Milcheva, Milva, Nicolesco, Noli, Oostwoud, Ravazzi, New Swingle Singers, Coro della RAI di Torino, cond. Berio. Sections from the opera were given separate performances before the work was completed under the titles *Pas de Quoi* (1st perf.: Cologne, 1978, WDR), *Scena* (1st perf.: Brussels, 1978, cond. Bartholomée.), *Studi* (1st perf.: Rome, 1979, Orchestra dell'Accademia di S.Cecilia, cond. Peskó), *Entrata* (1st perf.: San Francisco, 1980, San Francisco Symphony, cond. de Waart), *Suite* (1st perf.: Venice, 1981, cond. Panni), *Fanfara* (1st perf.: Venice, 1982, Orchestra Sinfonica della RAI). They have been re-absorbed into the opera.

1980–1

Accordo for four groups of wind instruments (2 piccolos, 2 flutes, oboe, 3 clarinets, soprano, alto and tenor saxophones,—2 horns, 2 trumpets, 2 trombones, 2 each of soprano, alto, tenor and baritone flugelhorns, 3 bass tubas—percussion). UE 1st perf.: Assisi, 1980.

Corale on Sequenza VIII for violin, two horns, and strings. UE 1st perf.: Zurich, 1982, Chiarappa, Collegium Musicum Zürich, cond. Sacher.

1982

Duo (Calvino) '*teatro immaginario*' for radio, for baritone (Sarti), two violins (Chiarappa, Tacchi), choir, and orchestra (Orchestra Sinfonica e Coro della RAI di Torino cond. Berio) on tape. UE 1st perf.: RAI, Rome, 1982. Winner of the 34th Premio Italia, 1982. A study for *Un re in ascolto*.

1979–83

34 duetti for two violins. UE 1st perf.: (of 27 of them) Fiesole, 1981. 1st complete perf.: Los Angeles, 1984.

1983

Lied for clarinet. UE 1st perf.: Kanoff, Geneva, 1983.

1979–84

Un re in ascolto (Calvino, Auden, Gotter, Berio) '*azione musicale*' in two parts for four sopranos, two mezzo-sopranos, three tenors, baritone, bass-baritone, two basses, actor, singing pianist, chorus (SATB), mimes, dancers, acrobats, pianist, accordion player, and orchestra (3 flutes, 2 oboes, cor anglais, Eb clarinet, 2 Bb clarinets, bass clarinet, saxophone, 2 bassoons, double bassoon—3 horns, 3 trumpets, 3 trombones, tuba—celesta, electric organ, percussion—strings). UE 1st perf.: Salzburg, 1984, Adam, Armstrong, Gonda, Greenberg, Harrap, Ionescu, Lohner, Molcho, Moser, Muff, Sima, Tichy, Wildhaber, Wise, Yachmi, Zednik, Wiener Philharmoniker, cond. Maazel (A concert version, produced in 1985–6, has since been withdrawn).

1984

Voci for viola and two groups of instruments (A: flute, cor anglais, clarinet, bass clarinet, bassoon—horn, trumpet, trombone—1 percussionist—3 violins, 3 violas, 3 cellos, 3 double basses; B: 2 flutes, oboe, Eb clarinet, Bb clarinet, bassoon—horn, trumpet, trombone, bass tuba—2 percussionists—electric organ—9 violins, 2 violas, 3 cellos, double bass). UE 1st perf.: Basle, 1984, Bennici, Basler Sinfonie-Orchester, cond. Berio.
Sequenza X for trumpet in C and piano resonance. UE 1st perf.: Los Angeles, 1984, Stevens.

1984–5

Requies for orchestra (piccolo, flute, oboe, cor anglais, Eb clarinet, Bb clarinet, bass clarinet, 2 bassoons—2 horns, 2 trumpets, trombone—marimbaphone, celesta, harp—strings). UE 1st perf. of incomplete version, entitled *Requies: Frammento (in memoriam Cathy)*: Lausanne, 1984, cond. Jordan. 1st complete perf.: Aspen, 1985, Aspen Music Festival Orchestra, cond. Berio. Revised 1987.

1985

Call—St. Louis Fanfare for brass quintet (2 trumpets, horn, trombone, tuba). UE 1st perf.: St Louis, 1985, Nashville Contemporary Brass Quintet. Revised 1987.
Luftklavier for piano. UE 1st perf.: Italy, 1985, Nardi.

1985–6

Naturale for viola, tam-tam, and recorded voice (Celano). UE. 1st perf.: Taormina, 1985, Bennicci.

Ricorrenze for wind quintet. UE 1st perf.: Darmstadt, 1987, Quintetto Arnold.

Formazioni for orchestra (4 flutes (plus 2 piccolos), 2 oboes, cor anglais, E♭ clarinet, 2 B♭ clarinets, bass clarinet, alto and tenor saxophone, 6 horns, 4 trumpets, 4 trombones, 2 tubas—3 percussionists—celesta (plus electronic organ), 2 harps—strings (12.12.12.10.8)). UE 1st perf.: Amsterdam, 1987, Concertgebouw Orchestra cond. Chailly. Subsequently extended. 1st perf. of final version: Amsterdam, 1988, same forces.

Sequenza XI for guitar. UE 1st perf.: Rovereto, 1988, Fisk.

Canticum novissimi testamenti (Sanguineti) ballata for choir (SATB). UE 1st perf.: 1988, Trent, I Minipolifonici.

Ofanim (Ezekiel and Song of Songs) for female voice, two children's choirs, two instrumental groups, and TRAILS sound location system. UE 1st perf.: Prato, 1988, Kenan, Finchley Children's Music Group, Concentus Musicus, cond. Berio. Various other versions of *Ofanim* were subsequently tried, bearing different numbers. These have now been withdrawn in favour of the original formation.

Concerto II (Echoing Curves) for piano and two instrumental groups (A: 3 flutes, oboe, cor anglais, 3 clarinets, bass clarinet, saxophone, 2 bassoons, double bassoon—2 horns, 2 trumpets, 2 trombones, bass tuba—celesta—3 violas, 3 cellos, 3 double basses; B: piccolo, oboe, E♭ clarinet, alto saxophone, D trumpet, C trumpet, 3 horns, trombone, 2 violins, 6 violas, 4 cellos, 4 double basses— electric organ). UE 1st perf.: Paris, 1988, Barenboim. Subsequently revised and extended. Incorporates a reworking of *Points on the Curve to Find.. . .* (1974) as its central section.

Rendering, 'Restoration of Fragments from a Symphony by Franz Schubert' for orchestra (2 flutes, 2 oboes, 2 clarinets, 2 bassoons —2 horns, 2 trumpets, 3 trombones—timpani, celesta—strings). UE 1st perf.: (of first two movements) Amsterdam, 1989, Concertgebouw Ochestra, cond. Harnoncourt.

1989

Calmo for mezzo-soprano and small orchestra (flute, alto flute, E♭ clarinet, 2 B♭ clarinets, bass clarinet, alto saxophone, bassoon—horn, 2 trumpets, trombone—harp—3 violas, 3 cellos, 2 double-basses—percussion). Recomposition of *Calmo* (1974).

Cantiam Novissimi Testamenti II (Sanguineti) for eight voices, clarinet quartet, and saxophone quartet. UE 1st perf.: Paris, 1989, cond. Bonlez.

Festum for orchestra. UE 1st perf.: Dallas, 1989, Dallas Symphony Orchestra.

Feuerklavier for piano. 1st perf.: New York, 1989, Serkin.

TRANSCRIPTIONS

1966

Il combattimento di Tancredi e Clorinda, Monteverdi, arranged for soprano, tenor, baritone, three violas, cello, double-bass, and harpsichord. UE 1st perf.: New York, 1967, Titus, Mandac, cond. Berio.

1967

Le grand lustucru (from *Marie galante*), Weill, arranged for mezzo-soprano and instruments (flute (plus piccolo), oboe, 2 clarinets, bassoon—2 trumpets—percussion—solo strings). UE 1st perf.: Venice, 1967, Berberian.

Surabaya Johnny (from *Happy End*), Weill, arranged for mezzo-soprano and instruments (flute, clarinet, trumpet, percussion, guitar, solo strings). UE 1st perf.: Venice, 1967, Berberian.

Song of Sexual Slavery (Brecht, translated by Berberian) (from *Die Dreigroschenoper*), Weill, arranged for mezzo-soprano and instruments (clarinet, bass clarinet, vibraphone, accordion, solo strings). UE 1st perf.: Venice, 1967, Berberian.

Michelle, McCartney and Lennon, arranged (i) for voice, 2 flutes, harpsichord; (ii) for voice, flute, clarinet, harp, violin, viola, cello, double-bass. 1st perf. (though of which version is not clear): Venice, 1967, Berberian.

Ticket to Ride, McCartney and Lennon, arranged for voice, flute, oboe, trumpet, violin, viola, cello, double bass, and harpsichord. 1st perf.: Venice, 1967, Berberian.

Yesterday, McCartney and Lennon, arranged for voice, flute, and harpsichord. 1st perf.: Venice, 1967, Berberian.

1978

Siete canciones populares españolas, de Falla, arranged for mezzo-soprano and orchestra (2 flutes, oboe, cor anglais, 3 clarinets, 2 bassoons, double bassoon—2 horns, 2 trumpets, 2 trombones, tuba—timpani, castanets, percussion—strings). UE 1st perf.: Italy, 1978, Berberian, cond. Berio.

1986

Brahms–Berio Op. 120 No. 1, for clarinet or viola and orchestra (2 flutes, 2 oboes, 2 clarinets, 2 bassoons, double bassoon—3 horns, 2 trumpets, trombone—timpani—strings). UE 1st perf.: Los Angeles, 1986, Zukovsky, Los Angeles Philharmonic, cond. Lewis.

1986

Fünf frühe Lieder, Mahler, for male voice and orchestra (2 flutes (plus piccolo), oboe, cor anglais, 2 clarinets, bass clarinet, 2 bassoons, double bassoon—3 horns, 2 trumpets, trombone, tuba—timpani, percussion—harp—strings). UE 1st perf.:

Dobbiacco, 1986, Hampson, Orchestra Haydn di Bolzano e Trento, cond. Michael.

1987

Sechs frühe Lieder, Mahler, for baritone and orchestra (piccolo, 2 flutes, 2 oboes, cor anglais, Eb clarinet, 2 Bb clarinets, bass clarinet, 2 bassoons, double bassoon—4 horns, 4 trumpets, 3 trombones, tuba—timpani, 2 percussionists—harp, celesta—strings). UE 1st perf.: Reggio Emilia, 1987, Hampson, Orchestra Sinfonica dell'Emilia Romagna a. Toscanini, cond. Berio.

Wir bauen eine Stadt, Hindemith, for children and chamber orchestra (2 flutes, oboe, 2 clarinets, bass clarinet, 2 bassoons, double bassoon—2 horns, 2 trumpets, 2 trombones—2 percussionists—glockenspiel, harp, piano—strings). UE 1st perf.: Vienna, 1988, cond. Berio. (Also, versions for seven instrumentalists by Scogna, and two pianos by Berio).

UNFINISHED WORKS

A number of unfinished works have nevertheless found their way into Work Lists. They are as follows:

1945–6

L'Annunciazione (Rilke) for soprano and chamber orchestra.

1947–8

Due liriche di Garcia Lorca for bass and orchestra. Only one of these, 'Camino', was completed.

c.1949

Tema e Variazioni for chamber orchestra.

Quartetto for wind

Amores (Ottolenghi) for sixteen singers and fourteen instruments.

Fantasia after Gabrieli for orchestra. Unfinished arrangement. (A recorded performance for the RAI in 1977 was in fact not of this, but of an arrangement by Maderna. Also included in the concert was a *Toccata* for orchestra, after Frescobaldi by Ghedini, which has erroneously found a place in some Berio Work Lists).

OCCASIONAL WORKS

1964

Rounds for Harpsichord with Voice (Markus Kutter). Vocal part added for a recording by Vischer and Berberian. Subsequently withdrawn.

1968

Prayer-Prière (Calvino). For Stockhausen's fortieth birthday. 1st perf.: Paris, 1968, Berberian. Consisted only of text and written instructions. A fragment of the text was subsequently used as Ballata V, 'Che il canto faccia', from Part I of *La vera storia* (1977–81).

1969

The Modification and Instrumentation of a Famous Hornpipe as a Merry and Altogether Sincere Homage to Uncle Alfred, Purcell, arranged for flute or oboe, clarinet, percussion, harpsichord, viola, cello. 1st perf.: London, 1969, Pierrot Players, along with 10 compositions by other composers, in celebration of the eightieth birthday of Dr Kalmus.

1971

Autre fois: berceuse canonique pour Igor Stravinsky for flute, clarinet, and harp.

1974

Musica Leggera, canone per moto contrario e al rovescio, con un breve intermezzo for flute and viola, accompanied by cello. For Petrassi's seventieth birthday.

1975

Selezione for piano and chamber orchestra (2 flutes, 2 oboes, 2 clarinets, 2 bassoons—2 horns, 2 trumpets, tenor trombone—snare drum, 6 cencerros, marimbaphone—strings). 1st perf.: Milan, 1976, Canino, Orchestra da Camera della Scala, cond. Panni. Arranged for Bruno Canino from the *Concerto* for two pianos and orchestra (1972–3), and subsequently withdrawn.

1985

Mix (of materials from *Linea* (1973) and *Sequenza IX* (1979–80)). 1st perf.: Taormina, 1985 (for dance festival).

Terre Chaleureuse for wind quintet. For Pierre Boulez's sixtieth birthday. 1st perf.: 1985, SWF Baden-Baden. A first sketch for *Ricorrenze* (1985–7).

1987

Ecce: musica per musicologi (Guido d'Arezzo) for women's voices, men's voices, and bells. For the XIV Congress of the International Musicological Society. 1st perf.: 1987, Bologna, members of the International Musicological Society, cond. Berio.

Comma for E♭ clarinet. For François Lesure.

1989

Arrangement of Schubert's *An die Musik* for chorus and small orchestra. 1st perf.: 1989, Orchestre de Paris, cond. Solti.

BIBLIOGRAPHY

ALBÉRA, PHILIPPE, 'Introduction aux neuf Sequenzas', *Contrechamps*, i, *Luciano Berio*, (Lausanne, 1983), pp. 91–122.

ALTMANN, PETER, *Sinfonia von Luciano Berio: eine analytische Studie* (Universal Edition, Vienna, 1977).

ANHALT, ISTVAN, 'Berio's *Sequenza III*: A Portrait', in *Alternative Voices* (Univ. of Toronto Press, Toronto, 1984), pp. 25–40.

ANNIBALDI, CLAUDIO, 'Berio', *The New Grove Dictionary of Music and Musicians* (Macmillan, London, 1980), pp. 554–9.

AROM, SIMHA., 'The Use of Play-back Techniques in the Study of Oral Polyphonies'. *Ethnomusicology* 20/3, (1976).

BAKHTIN, MIKHAIL, *Tvorchestvo Fransua Rable* (Khudozhestvennia literatura, Moscow, 1965); English trans. (by Helene Iswolsky) *Rabelais and His World* (The M.I.T. Press, Cambridge, Massachusetts, 1968).

BARTHES, ROLAND, 'Ascolto', *Enciclopedia Einaudi* (Einaudi, Turin, 1976), pp. 982–91. French text in *L'Obvie et l'obtus* (Paris, 1982); English trans. (by Richard Howard) in *The Responsibility of Forms* (New York, 1985), pp. 245–60.

BERIO, LUCIANO, 'Aspetti di artigianato formale', *Incontri musicali: Quaderni internazionali di musica contemporanea*, i (Milan, 1956), pp. 55 ff. French trans. in *Contrechamps*, i, *Luciano Berio* (Lausanne, 1983), pp. 10–23.

—— 'Poesia e musica—un' esperienza', *Incontri musicali: Quaderni internazionali di musica contemporanea*, iii (Milan, 1959), pp. 98 ff. French trans. in *Contrechamps*, i, *Luciano Berio* (Lausanne, 1983), pp. 24–35.

—— 'Du geste et de Piazza Carità', *La Musique et ses problèmes contemporains, Cahiers Renaud-Barrault*, i (Paris, 1963). French trans. in *Contrechamps*, i, *Luciano Berio* (Lausanne, 1983), pp. 41–5.

—— *Two Interviews* (Marion Boyars, London, 1985). Trans. and ed. by David Osmond-Smith from *Intervista sulla musica* (Laterza, Bari, 1981) and *Beszélgetések Luciano Berioval* (Editio Musica, Budapest, 1981).

—— 'Eco in ascolto', *Contemporary Music Review*, 5 (1989), pp. 1–8.

CALVINO, ITALO 'Un re in ascolto' *Sotto il sole giaguaro* (Garzanti, Milan, 1986), pp. 59–92, trans. William Weaver, in *Under the Jaguar Sun* (Harcourt Brace Jovanovitch, New York, 1988).

CARPENTER, HUMPHREY, *W. H. Auden: A Biography* (Allen & Unwin, London, 1981).

DEMIERRE, JAQUES. ' "Circles": e. e. cummings lu par Luciano Berio', *Contrechamps*, i, *Luciano Berio* (Lausanne, 1983), pp. 123–80.

DONAT, MISHA, 'Berio and his "Circles" ', *Musical Times*, 105 (1964), p. 105.

—— 'Berio's "Sinfonia" ', *Listener*, 82 (1969), p. 89.

—— 'Forking Paths', *Listener*, 89 (1973), p. 125.

DRESSEN, NORBERT, *Sprache und Musik bei Luciano Berio: Untersuchungen zu seiner Vokalcompositionen* (Gustav Bosse, Regensburg, 1982).

ECO, UMBERTO, *Opera Aperta* (Bompiani, Milan, 1962).

FITZGERALD, T. A., 'A Study of the Sequenzas I to VII by Luciano Berio', M.Mus. thesis, Univ. of Melbourne, 1979.

FLYNN, GEORGE W, 'Listening to Berio's Music', *Musical Quarterly*, 61 (1975), pp. 388–421.

HICKS, MICHAEL, 'Text, Music, and Meaning in Berio's *Sinfonia*, 3rd Movement', *Perspectives of New Music*, 20 (1981–2), pp. 199–224.

International Phonetic Association, *The Principles of the International Phonetic Association* (IPA, London, 1949).

NERUDA, PABLO, *Selected Poems* (Penguin, Harmondsworth, 1975).

OSMOND-SMITH, DAVID, 'Berio in London', *Music and Musicians* (March 1975), pp. 16–19.

—— 'Berio and the Art of Commentary', *Musical Times*, 116 (1975), pp. 871–2.

—— 'From Myth to Music: Lévi-Strauss's *Mythologiques* and Berio's *Sinfonia*', *Musical Quarterly*, 67 (1981), pp. 230–60.

—— 'Joyce, Berio, et l'art de l'explosition', *Contrechamps*, i, *Luciano Berio* (Lausanne, 1983), pp. 83–9.

—— *Playing on Words: A Guide to Luciano Berio's* Sinfonia (Royal Musical Association, London, 1985).

—— 'Intimate Rapport: *Coro* and *Requies*', *Listener*, 114 (1985), p. 38.

—— 'Reinventing the Orchestra: *Concerto for Two Pianos and Formazioni*', *Listener*, 118 (1987), pp. 40–41.

—— 'Prospero's Peace: The Making of Berio's Opera *Un re in ascolto*', *Listener*, 121 (1989), pp. 34–5.

PESTALOZZA, LUIGI, 'Critica spettacolare della spettacolarità: conversazione con Edoardo Sanguineti' (on *Laborintus II* and *A-Ronne*), *Musica Realta* (June 1981), pp. 21–37.

POUSSEUR, HENRI, 'Outline of a Method', *Die Reihe*, iii, *Musical Craftsmanship* (Universal Edition, New Jersey, 1959), pp. 44–88 (orig. German edn.: Vienna, 1957).

RANDS, BERNARD, 'The Master of New Sounds', *Music and Musicians*, 19/12 (1971), p. 32.

SANGUINETI, EDOARDO, *Laborintus* (Magenta, Varese, 1956). Repr. in *Triperuno* (Feltrinelli, Milan, 1965).

—— 'Laborintus II', *Contrechamps*, i, *Luciano Berio* (Lausanne, 1983), pp. 75–82.

SANTI, PIERO, 'Luciano Berio', *Die Reihe*, iv (Universal Edition, New Jersey, 1960), pp. 98–102 (orig. German edn.: Vienna, 1958).

SCHULTZ, ANDREW N., 'Compositional Idea and Musical Action: *Sequenze I–VII by Luciano Berio—An Analytical Study*', D.Phil. thesis, Univ. of Queensland, 1985.

SMITH BRINDLE, REGINALD, 'Maderna and Berio', *Listener*, 85 (1971) p. 761.

STACEY, PETER F. *Contemporary Tendencies in the Relationship of Music and Text with Special Reference to* Pli selon pli *(Boulez) and* Laborintus II *(Berio)*. British Music Theses (Garland Publishing, New York, forthcoming).

STOIANOVA, IVANKA, *Luciano Berio: Chemins en musique*, La Revue musicale (Paris, 1985).

TRUMPY, BALZ, 'Pensées sur la musique de Luciano Berio', *Musique en jeu*, 33 (1978), pp. 128–30.

INDEX

155

DATE DUE
